Baddesley Clinton Hall from the west.

THE CASTLES AND MOATED MANSIONS OF WARWICKSHIRE

Mike Salter

CONTENTS

A GLOSSARY OF TERMS

Ashlar   - Masonry of blocks with even faces and square edges.
Bailey   - An enclosure defended by palisades, walls, or moats.
Barbican   - Porch, tower, or enclosure defending a gateway.
Battlement   - A parapet with crenellations protecting a wall walk.
Crenellations   - Indentations in the top of a parapet.
Curtain Walls   - High stone walls around a castle bailey.
Hammerbeam   - Beam projecting from a wall to carry arched braces.
Jamb   - The side of a doorway, window, or other opening.
Keep   - A building or small court acting as a citadel.
Light   - A compartment of a window.
Machicolation   - Slots behind a parapet for dropping missiles.
Merlons   - The upstanding portions of a crenellated parapet.
Moat   - A ditch, wet or dry, around an enclosure.
Motte   - Steep mound, usually at least partly artificial.
Mullion   - A vertical member dividing the lights of a window.
Ogival Arch   - Arch of oriental origin with convex & concave curves.
Perpendicular   - Architectural style with vertical accents dominant.
Pilaster   - Flat buttress or pier attached to a wall.
Plinth   - The projecting base of a wall, battered or stepped.
Portcullis   - Gate designed to rise and fall in vertical grooves.
Postern   - A secondary gateway or back doorway.
Respond   - Half pier bonded to a wall to carry an arch.
Ringwork   - A small enclosure defended by a high rampart.
Tierceron   - A secondary rib in a vault of complex pattern.
Transom   - Horizontal member dividing top & bottom window lights.
Wall Walk   - A walkway on a wall top, protected by a parapet.

FURTHER READING

The Victoria County History of Warwickshire, several volumes.
Birmingham & West Midlands Archeological Society Transactions
The Buildings of Warwickshire, Nikolaus Pevsner, 1974
Norman Castles in Britain, Derek Renn, 1968
Medieval Archeology
Country Life

INTRODUCTION

This book is essentially about medieval buildings in Warwickshire which illustrate the old saying that an Englishman's home is his castle. Those which are described here either had a genuine dual purpose as both fortress and private residence or were basically domestic buildings which were given features normally associated with fortifications to display the owner's rank, power, or prestige.

The concept of a privately owned fortress cum residence was little known in England prior to the invasion of William, Duke of Normandy in 1066. He established in England the feudal system in which lords held numerous units of land called manors directly from the King in return for military service. The lords kept some manors for their own use but the majority were given to knights and lesser lords, again in return for military service. The veneer of French speaking Norman lords consolidated their fragile hold on the lands inhabited by the Saxon populace by building themselves fortified residences which they called castles. Some Saxon lords remained in power, however, at least for a while. The Domesday Book of 1086, King William's inquisition into land usage and tenure, shows that Warwickshire had an abnormally high number of Saxon sub-tenants. The Bagot family are thought to be amongst these. Edwin, the Saxon Earl of Mercia, remained neutral in 1066, and was allowed to stay in power until he rebelled in 1071 and was defeated and killed.

In the spring of 1068 King William took the precaution of having several new castles erected in the Midlands, one of them being at Warwick. These castles were not structures of mortared stone for the construction of which several years of peaceful conditions and large numbers of unavailable skilled masons would have been needed. Instead they were earthworks hastily built with the aid of Saxon slave labour and surmounted by stockades and timber buildings with thatched roofs. Each comprised an enclosed court called a bailey defended by a rampart, stockade, and ditch, and containing a hall, chapel, stables, barns, and workshops. At one end of the bailey was a high conical mound dominating the site and having on its summit a wooden two or three storey tower within a small palisaded court. This latter served as the lord's residence and citadel. Today we call such a citadel-cum-private suite a keep but this term is quite modern. In an era when a castle would have no other tower except perhaps for a modest structure over the gateway it was adequate for chroniclers simply to refer to the tower or the motte.

Warwick
Castle
Motte

3

William I installed Henry, younger son of Robert de Beaumont, as constable of Warwick Castle and in 1088 William II created Henry Earl of Warwick, giving him extra lands formerly part of the estate of the Saxon thegn Turchil of Arden. William II also gave Coventry to the Earl of Chester, and the castle there, although not mentioned until 1143, perhaps existed by 1100. During Henry I's reign (1100-35) his chamberlain Geoffrey de Clinton built a pair of low lying castles defended by pools and water filled ditches at Brandon and Kenilworth, whilst the de Montforts built Beaudesert Castle. This fortress was of a different type, having a strongly embanked inner enclosure (which modern historians call a ringwork) instead of a true motte. There seem to have been others at Morton Bagot, Aston Cantlow, and Ratley. A motte was later raised over the last. The castles of Seckington and Brinklow were probably built c1135-40 by the Earl of Leicester or his knights, Brailes was built by the Earl of Warwick and most of the other mottes in Warwickshire are likely to be of about the same period, their building being a result of a conflict between King Stephen and Henry I's daughter Empress Maud. The Earls of Chester and Warwick sided with Maud. Robert Marmion of Tamworth Castle caused them problems until he was killed when his horse fell into the ditch he had just had dug round Coventry Priory in defiance of the castle garrison. In 1148 the Earls of Leicester and Chester made a treaty which in effect demilitarised a wide zone around Leicester by limiting the number of castles allowed there.

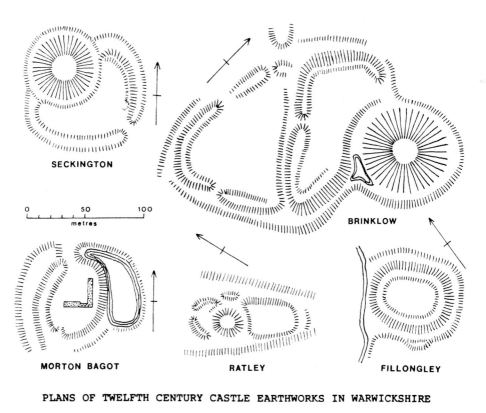

SECKINGTON

0   50   100
metres

BRINKLOW

MORTON BAGOT   RATLEY   FILLONGLEY

PLANS OF TWELFTH CENTURY CASTLE EARTHWORKS IN WARWICKSHIRE

4

The only possible evidence of construction in mortared stone at any Warwickshire castle prior to the 1180s is the crude gate tower base found by excavation at Ratley. Henry II restored order after his accession in 1154 but had problems with his sons in the 1170s. During this period Kenilworth was found to be useful to the Crown which obtained legal possession by an exchange of lands with the de Clintons. The keep and inner bailey walls were probably begun c1182. The keep is a particularly large and massive example of its type. There are only about a dozen medieval towers still standing in Britain that can rival it for size. It may enclose the original motte. This would explain the unusually deep multi-stepped plinth which in turn gives a secure base for square corner turrets of an unusual size and degree of projection. In fact among British keeps they are matched really only by the series of 13th century round corner towered keeps in Ireland and 14th century English buildings at Stafford, Dudley, and Langley in Northumberland. There were just two main rooms connected by a spiral stair in one turret and lit by narrow slit windows in deeply splayed round arched embrasures. A forebuilding contained the stair from the court to the doorway into the uppermost room and there were smaller rooms in the corner turrets. The only other work of this period in Warwickshire appears to be the original curtain wall at Warwick of which little remains.

King John (1199-1216) visited Kenilworth frequently, enclosing the outer bailey with a wall, improving the water defences, and perhaps also completing the keep. The outer wall had several towers varying in plan from a round to an octagon on a square base. The keep at Brandon probably built c1210-20 has an unusual plan with very thick end walls projecting beyond the thin side walls.

The Keep, Kenilworth Castle

The Water Tower, Kenilworth Castle

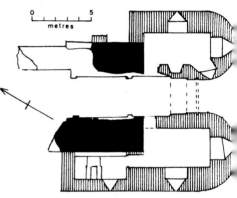

shell keep, Warwick Castle

PLAN OF MORTIMER'S TOWER, KENILWOR

Henry III carried on with the works at Kenilworth. Probably it was he who added twin drum towers in front of the square gatehouse. In 1227 the castle was a solitary bastion of royal authority when Henry quarrelled with his brother Richard, Earl of Cornwall, and the Earls of Warwick, Chester, and Derby, who between them were the overlords of almost all the manors in Warwickshire, supported the latter. It was probably about this time that the palisade around the motte summit at Warwick was replaced by polygonal wall forming what modern writers call a shell keep. Only part of it now remains and nothing has survived of the curtain wall and towers of c1250 at Peter de Montfort's castle of Beaudesert.

Kenilworth was eventually given to Henry III's sister and her husband Simon de Montfort, created Earl of Leicester. It became a centre of resistance when Simon led the barons against Henry, who was captured at the battle of Lewes in 1264. Henry's son Edward, who was held captive at Kenilworth late in 1264, had revenge during the following year when Earl Simon was killed in battle at Evesham. However the Earl's sons continued to hold the castle, and it was only after Henry had spent an entire year preparing for a siege and then actually conducting it that the garrison yielded on favourable terms. The water defences had proved so effective that even though the whole might of the kingdom was pitted against the castle only starvation enabled its capture. Warwick and Brandon castles were involved in these conflicts too, being ignominiously captured and destroyed by a sally of the rebel garrison at Kenilworth. Brandon was never restored and Warwick was not refortified until the 1360s.

6

Astley
Castle

The period of peace and stable government from 1266 until the death of Edward I in 1307, though a busy period for castle building in some counties, has left few relics in Warwickshire. From John's reign onwards it was normal for the Crown to licence the building of embattled walls and towers. Thus eventually they became status symbols even when not actually militarily necessary because such licences were only granted to a loyal privileged few. Walls and towers with surrounding wet moats were built around manor houses on flat sites at Weoley and Astley in response to licences granted by Henry III in the 1260s. Weoley has the lower parts of the walls and square towers around a semi-rectangular court now revealed by excavation. One square tower and some featureless walling remain at Astley, where the moat still partly contains water.

Weoley
Castle

7

Moated site near Lapworth Park

Like most English counties Warwickshire has many rectangular or nearly rectangular moated enclosures which mark the sites of former manor houses. They are particularly common in the Forest of Arden in the north of the county. A few have modest stone walls on the inner edge of the moat, or ranges of buildings without towers or battlements set round a central court, as at Baddesley Clinton, but the majority had only a hedge or fence on the inner side of the moat with a house isolated inside often partly built of timber or even wattle and daub. Some were later superseded by farmhouses of more durable materials set either within the platform or beyond it.

Although a fair amount of excavation and research has been done on the Forest of Arden moats in the last 30 years some questions remain unanswered. It seems that some moats are as early as the 12th century, but the majority date from the 13th and 14th centuries, perhaps a response to the periods of unrest in the reigns of Henry III, Edward II, and Richard II, although the Forest of Arden moats are now thought to be associated with the reclamation of wasteland by men of lesser rank who moated their houses as a means of showing the rank they aspired to. Quite a number of moats seem to have been disused after 1400, although fresh moats of the 15th century and later are known. Sometimes they occur in groups of two or three because of manors being split between heiresses or the abandonment of one site in favour of another near by. Some were only occupied for a generation or two. Others have been in continuous occupation.

A water filled ditch around a manor house was not necessarily military in purpose although if the only access across it was by a drawbridge it formed a useful barrier, the mud at the bottom being as much an obstacle as the water, which was often not very deep. A moat permanently and efficiently kept out vagrants, wild animals, and malefactors, and kept in domestic animals, servants, and the household children. At all periods moats have been appreciated as scenic features and they served as a habitat for fish, eels, and water fowl, which together formed a substantial part of the medieval diet. A wet moat could also help to drain land otherwise unsuited for habitation and would serve to flush latrines draining into it. Because of the many uses to which they were put moats did not need royal consent of the sort required for embattled walls and towers. However, they still functioned as status symbols as only manorial lords and the more wealthy parochial clergy possessed the land and wealth needed for their creation.

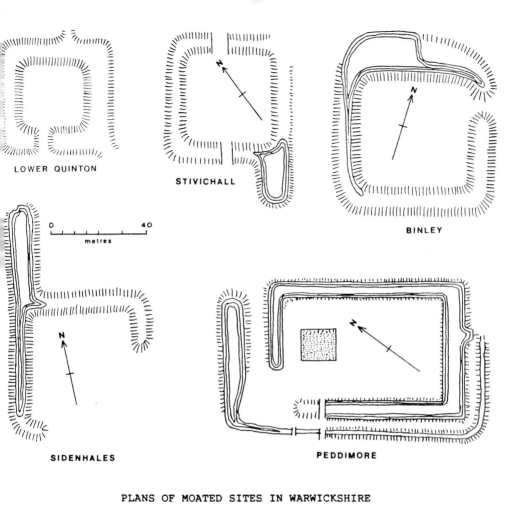

LOWER QUINTON

STIVICHALL

BINLEY

SIDENHALES

PEDDIMORE

0   40

metres

PLANS OF MOATED SITES IN WARWICKSHIRE

A few comments need making about domestic buildings and their features. Glass was uncommon in medieval secular buildings, windows being closed with shutters so the rooms were dark when the weather was bad. Fireplaces were often provided in the walls but some rooms had central hearths with louvres in the roof. Window embrasures might have stone seats but movable furnishings were sparse and simple as lords tended to circulate from one castle or manor house to another to consume agricultural produce in situ. Their servants and a few portable furnishings went with them leaving only caretakers. Only in time of war would there be a permanent garrison. Iron stanchions secured wide openings within reach of the ground. Internal walls were often plastered and painted with allegorical or biblical scenes or patterns. External walls were sometimes whitewashed unless they were of ashlar. By the 14th century private rooms with latrines and fireplaces were provided in towers and ranges of timber or stone set against the curtain walls, but originally there was hardly any privacy and some household members would bed down in the places in which they worked like the kitchen or stables, or in the main hall.

9

Hartshill Castle from the east

The 14th century was a boom period for castle building in the county of Warwickshire. The initial stimulus for building defences was the disturbed state of the country under Edward II. It seems that the district of Arden lived in fear of John de Somery, Lord of Dudley Castle. Little or nothing remains of several of the castles such as Beauchamp's Court, Langley, Ragley, and Whichford, but at Maxstoke is one of England's best preserved lesser fortresses of this period. It has a medium sized rectangular court with four low octagonal corner towers plus a gatehouse with octagonal turrets and a wet moat around the whole. The main apartments lay in a range set on the opposite side from the gateway with other ranges, now gone, on the other two sides. Maxstoke was a de Clinton seat, replacing those lost to them at Kenilworth and Brandon.

Great Hall & Strong Tower, Kenilworth Castle

Guy's Tower, Warwick Castle   *Caesar's Tower, Warwick Castle*

A former motte and bailey site at Hartshill was refortified with a thin curtain wall with crossloops at intervals, and two sections of wall with a small polygonal corner tower remain at Kingsbury. Caludon has just a fragment of walling pierced by windows which are likely to have served the main hall. The hall at Kenilworth was in 1347 re-roofed, but in the 1380s it was entirely reconstructed for John of Gaunt, Duke of Lancaster, in the Perpendicular architectural style then coming into fashion. Although ruined Lancaster's work at Kenilworth, which included sumptuous private apartments, two high towers set at either end of the hall, an elaborate entrance porch and steps, and a huge kitchen, is amongst the best secular work of its period in Britain. Competing with it, and better preserved, are the new outer defences at Warwick. There the Beauchamps rebuilt the bailey walls in c1360-94 and provided the NE front with a fine gatehouse with a barbican in the middle and a lofty machicolated tower at each end. In plan these towers are very unusual, one being tri-lobed and the other twelve sided. Although they contained some useful rooms and served to flank and command the curtain walls it is clear they were built for show as status symbols of lordly rank and power, the Beauchamps now being not only Earls of Warwick and pre-eminent in the county, but among the leading men of the land. They also provided a fine range of apartments but only the cellars of these have survived later rebuilding.

Baginton has just the overgrown basement remaining of a strange structure which seems to have been a self contained two storey hall and solar block forming a sort of tower house although such towers normally have at least three storeys with the private room set over the hall instead of beside it.

Richard III Tower, Warwick

Little 15th century work, domestic or military, remains in the castles. In 1412 an older moated house at Fulbrook was improved both in terms of the accommodation and picturesqueness by the addition of a gatehouse. Only a decade later the building was superseded by a new nearby mansion faced at least partly with brick. Neither now survive except for some featureless masonry perhaps representing the former. Henry V built a moated timber summer house called The Pleasance at the far end of the lake at Kenilworth. The domestic ranges at Maxstoke were remodelled in the late 15th century. There are gunports in the porch adjoining one of the ranges of c1485 at Baddesley Clinton. Probably they were copied from the rectangular tower with octagonal corner turrets begun by Richard III at Warwick and left unfinished when he was defeated and killed at Bosworth in 1485. It was evidently intended as a self contained tower house similar to others built by other leading Yorkists in the period of their ascendancy from 1461 to 1485 at Raglan, Ashby, and elsewhere.

By the late 15th century cannon had developed to a degree which endangered high stone walls and towers. They increasingly became to be regarded as status symbols offering a defence only against rebel tenants or light bodies of infantry. New moated mansions like Compton Wyniates, a thinly walled brick structure of the 1520s, or the gatehouse at Coughton Court of the 1520s on an earlier base, have no military value but were designed to be as showy as possible with a deliberate intention towards the picturesque. Crenellation remained an important symbol of status and royal favour. As late as 1567 a licence was granted for crenellating Mountgrevill House.

There are or were 16th century domestic ranges at many of the castles and moated mansions. Henry VIII added a kitchen at Warwick and a timber range was erected to accommodate Queen Elizabeth I in 1572. The Earl of Leicester, the Queen's favourite, went further to please her at Kenilworth. He built a four storey apartment block and a new gatehouse with octagonal corner turrets. Little remains of the house of this period at Hartshill. More survives of a house of c1500 and later at Kingsbury. In James I's time transformation of the decayed apartments at Warwick into a splendid palace began.

Leicester's improvements at Kenilworth so weakened the outer defences that during the Civil War of the 1640s a royalist garrison was withdrawn and it was taken over by Parliament which already had garrisons at Maxstoke and Warwick. The latter withstood an attack by the Earl of Northampton in 1643. The Earl was killed later in the war and his house at Compton was among several which suffered from raids and plundering. Lord Brooke of Warwick was another war casualty, killed storming Lichfield Cathedral Close in 1643.

Maxstoke and Warwick managed to avoid being slighted after the war and although their domestic ranges have been subsequently much altered the main defences are nearly intact. Kenilworth was made untenable and is now much ruined except for Leicester's gatehouse which is still inhabited. The apartments at Astley, rebuilt c1580-1620, survived intact until ruination very recently. The mansions at Coughton, Compton Wyniates, and Baddesley Clinton remain mostly intact although only Baddesley is still fully moated. Other moated sites have either lost their medieval buildings or have seen them altered and extended out of recognition as at New Hall. At Weoley excavations in the 1950s revealed the bases of all the walls and earlier excavations revealed the lower parts of the tower house at Baginton and keep at Brandon. The latter is now buried again. Only earthworks and very minor fragments survive elsewhere.

Remnant of shell keep converted into an 18th Century folly, Warwick Castle

GAZETTEER OF CASTLES AND MOATED MANSIONS

ALLESLEY CASTLE
SP 304804

Nothing now remains of this castle built by the Hastings family in the early 14th century. They held Allesley from the mid 13th century until 1389, when it passed to Lord Bergavenny. The castle was just a site by the 1580s when Robert Fitch held the manor, but traces of the moat were still visible until the 19th century.

ARROW MOTTE
SP 084559

The barely discernable motte on an outlying ridge of Primrose Hill above the east bank of the River Arrow is perhaps a relic of Robert Marmion's campaigns in support of King Stephen in the 1140s.

ASTLEY CASTLE
SP 313894

Astley was long held by a family who took their name from the manor here they held from the Earls of Warwick. After Thomas de Astley died fighting for Simon de Montfort at Evesham in 1265, Astley was given to Warine de Bassingburn who in 1266 was licenced to enclose the house with a moat and crenellated wall. However, Thomas's son Andrew had recovered his estates by the end of that year. Probably it was he who built a stone curtain wall around the oval platform 75m by 57m and surrounded it with a wet moat with a nearly square outer perimeter.

When Sir William de Astley died in 1420 the castle went to his daughter Joan, married to Reynald, Lord Grey of Ruthin. The first husband of Elizabeth Woodville, who married Edward IV in 1464, was one of their descendants, who intermarried with the Staffords. In 1554, when he was executed after his daughter Lady Jane Grey's nine day reign, Henry, Duke of Stafford held Astley. Queen Mary is said to have destroyed the castle. She gave Astley to Edward Chamberlain and it was subsequently leased to various families until sold to Sir Richard Newdigate, who died in 1678. Sir Roger Newdigate, d1806, was the last of the direct male line although the Parkers assumed the Newdigate name on succeeding to Astley.

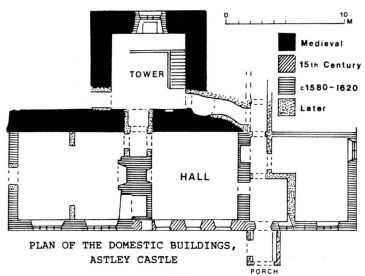

PLAN OF THE DOMESTIC BUILDINGS,
ASTLEY CASTLE

Astley Castle from the SW

The complex architectural history of Astley Castle has yet to be unravelled. Only overgrown fragments remain of the curtain wall overlooking the moat. The gutted range of apartments served as a hotel as recently as the late 1970s. The main block is 30m long and seems to incorporate a straight length of walling 1.8m thick not forming part of the outer perimeter, with the stump of a projecting tower 10m square, the interior of which was later adapted to take the main staircase. The tower has signs of a former spiral stair in the east corner. The central section of the 8m wide range built against these older parts retains three 15th century windows from a hall which was shortened during a remodelling in the period 1580-1630. Then, or later, the range was doubled in width at the SW end with a new NW wall flush with that of the older tower, and it was given an embattled parapet. The porch and various internal walls are 18th and 19th century.

ASTON CANTLOW CASTLE   SP 137600

The Cantilupes had their chief residence at Aston until William de Cantilupe married Eva de Braose in the 13th century, thus obtaining several Welsh Border castles. There are faint fraces of a ringwork or moated platform beside the River Alne west of the village.

BILLESLEY MOAT   SP 148568

Three arms of a moat still full of water remain south of the church, the lane to which has been built on the filled in west side. Osbert Trussell held the manor in 1166 from the Botilers. Except for short periods of forfeiture for rebellion against King John, Henry III, and Edward II, Trussells lived here until the attainder of Thomas in 1588 after his execution for a highway robbery in Kent. However from the late 13th century their principal seat was Acton Trussell in Staffordshire. During the long minority of Avery Trussell during the 1520s Richard Fulwood let the house at Billesley fall into decay. Part was demolished and later the present house was built. It later passed through various families, notably the Whalleys, Sherlocks, Gooches, Youngs, and Mills.

Baddesley
Clinton
Hall

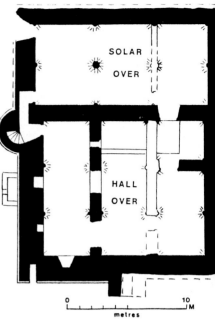

PLAN OF BAGINTON CASTLE

BADDESLEY CLINTON HALL

SP 200714

The moat is thought to have been dug by Sir Thomas de Clinton, who in 1290 married the Besege heiress to Baddesley. It passed to the Coningsbys after Leonard de Clinton died in 1349, and was conveyed to Robert Burdet in 1400. In 1438 the hall was bought by the Warwick lawyer John Brome. His houses in Warwick and Baddesley were broken into by malefactors one day in June 1450, and he was murdered in London by the Earl of Warwick's Steward John Herthill in 1468. His son Nicholas in turn murdered Herthill in 1471. Nicholas died in 1517, leaving a daught who married Sir Edward Ferrers. In 1980 the Ferrers family sold Baddesley to the government which conveyed it to the National Trust for preservation as an ancient monument.

The hall originally had four ranges measuring 32m by 26m overall lying within a wet moat 9m wide with fishponds beyond to the NW. The original hall lay in the vanished NW range, and a new hall was provided in the SE range as rebuilt by Henry Ferrers in the 1580s. Brick replaced timber framing in the outer walls in the first half of the 18th century. The other ranges are mostly of the 1480s, but the SW range has a short piece of 14th century walling close to the turret on the south corner. The NE range contains the entrance via a porch with keyhole shaped gunports. A brick bridge has replaced a former drawbridge. The room over the gate was remodelled by Henry Ferrers and given a big new six-light window. The battlements over it are Victorian. The SW range was widened towards the court c1890.

BAGINTON CASTLE

Sir Richard Herthill sold Baginton to Sir Richard Bagot who built the present castle on the site of an older house. It was probably completed in time for the visit of Henry, Duke of Hereford, prior to his intended combat with the Duke of Norfolk in 1397. Shakespeare immortalised Bagot as one of the agents Richard II left behind to raise funds by dubious means when the King went to Ireland in 1399. Bagot left a daughter, Isabel, who married Thomas Stafford, but in 1417 the castle was sold to the Earl of Warwick. It remained part of the Earldom until conveyed to the Dean and Chapter of St Mary's collegiate church at Warwick in 1471. When the college was closed in 1544 Baginton went to the Gooderes but was sold to the Bromleys in 1618. It is doubtful if the castle was much used after the time of the Bagots and Leland describes it as desolate in c1540.

The castle lies on the end of a ridge above the River Soar west of the village. It was actually set below the summit of the ridge from which it seems to have been divided by a broad and deep moat, now filled in on the north side where the ground is much disturbed. Of the buildings of a court about 40m square there remain only the outer part of a small rectangular tower overlooking the river. Set within the moat on the east side are the overgrown and very ruined basements of a block which evidently contained a hall and chamber side by side on the vanished upper storey. The high quality ashlar faced walling is from 1.6m to 2.0m thick and has responds and piers for quadripartite vaulting. The hall was probably entered from the court by a drawbridge or timber ramp. The space below it measures 13.6m by 11m, and that below the chamber 14.4m by 6.6m. A rounded mid-wall turret contained a stair linking the two levels and there were latrines in a rectangular block on the south and at the SW corner. Probably the building was double-gabled within a parapet. The remains were only exposed to view by excavations in the 1930s.

Baginton Castle

*Beaudesert
Castle*

BEAUCHAMP'S COURT

SP 085586

This was the house of the manor of Alcester, lying NW of the town.
In 1272 Walter de Beauchamp purchased half of the manor from the
de Botreaux or Botterell family, and the other half was purchased
from Thomas Botreaux in 1444 by Sir John Beauchamp of Powick. Giles,
younger son of Walter, in 1340 obtained a licence from Edward III
to crenellate the house and surround it with a wall of stone and
lime. In the 1530s the manor passed by marriage to Fulke Greville.
In 1545 Leland reported that Fulke was rebuilding 'Beauchamp's
Hawle' with materials from recently dissolved Alcester Priory. It
remained the Grenville chief seat until a later Sir Fulke, created
Baron Brooke of Beauchamp's Court in 1621, obtained and remodelled
Warwick Castle. The Court was neglected and left empty after the
death of William Greville, the last occupant, in 1653. Part of the
house was demolished in 1667 and the remainder was let as a farm.
Only a very overgrown moated platform now remains.

BEAUDESERT CASTLE

SP 155662

Henry de Newburgh, Earl of Warwick, gave part of Preston Bagot to
his great nephew Thurstan de Montfort who built a castle on those
lands, calling them Beaudesert (beautiful wasteland). He obtained a
charter for a market beside the castle from the Empress Maud c1140.
It was perhaps his great grandson Peter, who succeeded in 1216 and
was killed alongside his kinsman the Earl of Leicester in 1265, who
walled in the inner bailey in stone. Possibly there was a slightly
earlier tower keep too, but nothing of either now remain. When his
grandson Peter died in 1369 the castle reverted to Thomas, Earl of
Warwick as overlord. The manor was held by Lord Bergavenny from
1376 to 1410 and then the Botillers of Sudeley until sold to Edward
IV in 1477, but the castle may have been retained by the Earls of
Warwick. The last mention of work on it is a minor repair to the
porch of the hall in 1411. It is not mentioned in a survey of 1547
and all the stonework had gone, probably for building at Henry-in-
Arden nearby, by Dugdale's time. The ridge on which the castle was
built is quite a good defensive site. An oval ringwork 77m by 54m
rising up to 10m above the surrounding ditch lies near the NE end
of the ridge, leaving room for just a triangular barbican beyond.
Extending in line to the SW are two outer enclosures of similar
size to the inner ward with a ditch between them. It is unlikely
that the outer enclosures were ever walled in stone but parts of a
13th or 14th century moulded capital were found in the inner ward in
the 1840s, and wooden water pipes were removed in the 1850s.

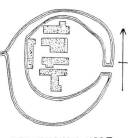

BIRMINGHAM MOAT

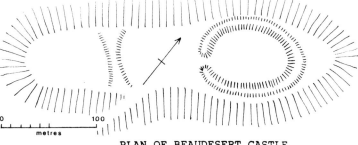

PLAN OF BEAUDESERT CASTLE

BILLESLEY MOAT
SP 148568

Three arms of a water filled moat near the church mark the site of a house of the Trussells. Except for short periods of forfeiture they lived here from at least the time of Osbert Trussell in c1166 until the execution and attainder of Thomas Trussell for a highway robbery in Kent in 1588. However, from the late 13th century onward their chief seat was in Staffordshire, and during Avery Trussell's minority in the 1520s Richard Fulwood let the house fall into decay. Part was later demolished, then a new house was built nearby.

BIRMINGHAM MOAT
SP 074865

The manor of Birmingham was long held by a family of knights who took their name from the place, which they held under a series of overlords. In 1166 Peter de Birmingham, son of William, Steward of Dudley, was authorised to hold a market at his castle of Birmingham. After William de Birmingham was killed fighting on the de Montfort side at the battle of Evesham in 1265 he was disinherited and Roger de Clifford had possession for a while, but a later William de Birmingham recovered the manor in c1302. A year before his death in 1425 the ninth William de Birmingham was ejected from the manor by Sir Edmund Ferrers during a dispute over ownership of it.

Edward Birmingham was the last resident lord of the manor. He got into debt as a result of insufficient supervision while still a minor, was convicted of a felony, and in 1536 surrendered the manor to Henry VIII in return for a pension. In 1557 the manor was granted to Thomas Marrow, whose descendents sold it in 1746 to the Archer family. However, these families let the property and a new house was built in c1740 for the manufacturer John Francis, although some medieval outbuildings then still survived.

The buildings had all gone by 1816, when the moat was filled in and the Smithfield Market built on the site. This in turn was demolished in 1959, and the opportunity was taken to excavate part of the site before redevelopment. Footings of an ashlar faced wall of a hall or range of apartments were found on the western part of the site. Dating evidence was inconclusive, but the middle third of the 13th century, or the early 14th, are the most likely periods for its construction. Hanson's 1778 plan of Birmingham shows five separate structures standing in the western half of a platform with an average diameter of about 65m. The moat was about 10m wide on the north and east, but wider on the other sides. The site lies on the southern half of the quadrangle now enclosed by Jamaica Row, Moat Row, Moat Lane, and St Martin's Lane, being only 100m SE of St Martin's Church. Hanson also shows a wet moat about 8m wide around a platform roughly 30m in diameter on which stood the parsonage. This lay across what it now the north end of Pershore St, close to where it joins Edgebaston St, some 200m SW of St Martin's Church.

BRAILES CASTLE

The manor was held by the Crown until granted in 1130 to the Earl
of Warwick. So the castle earthworks perched on a hillock with wide
views in all directions except to the north probably date c1135-40.
A park is mentioned in 1279 but the castle seems to have then been
out of use. A mound now about 4m high and 25m across on top lies in
the middle of a pear shaped platform about 90m long by 60m wide.

BRANDON CASTLE
SP 408759

Geoffrey de Clinton had a castle here by the 1150s. It later went
to Nicholas de Verdon. Coins found during excavations suggest that
he built the stone keep during King John's reign and in 1226 it is
recorded that he raised the level of the extensive moats fed from
the adjacent River Avon. His son John supported Henry III during
his struggles with de Montfort. In 1266 Brandon Castle was captured
by the garrison of Kenilworth in a surprise sortie and burnt. It
does not appear to have ever been restored.

The earthworks comprise two moated platforms about 85m by 60m
and 50m by 35m. To the north and west are traces of much larger
outer enclosures. The eastern corner of the larger platform has a
ditch dividing it off, and upon it was the keep. As revealed by an
excavation this was shown to have an unusual plan. Overall it was
a rectangle of 16.8m by 12.6m with end walls up to 4.5m thick with
a wide spiral stair in the SW corner. The side walls would have
been 3.3m thick but were in fact recessed either side of a central
buttress which may have carried arches at a higher level. The two
southern recesses may have served as shoots for latrines higher up.
The entrance was probably in the north wall.

Site of keep, Brandon Castle

20

Moat, Brandon Castle

BRINKLOW CASTLE

SP 439797

Though probably built by the Earl of Leicester the castle was held from the Earl by the Mowbrays until William de Stuteville obtained it after a lawsuit. Hugh Wake of Liddel married the heiress Joan de Stuteville, d1276, but under their descendants Brinklow was mostly held by tenants of which the Whittlebury family were most notable. By then the Earl of Lancaster was overlord. There are no traces of stonework but there are impressive earthworks of a pair of baileys 180m by 100m overall with high ramparts and deep ditches and at the east end is a lofty motte with a summit about 20m across on top.

BUSHWOOD HALL

SP 176692

A rectangular moat lies around a house of Queen Anne's reign. There is a record of Sir John Bishopesdon agreeing with a mason in 1313 for the construction of a hall 10m long above a gateway, but the moat was probably dug for a former owner, the Bishop of Worcester.

BUTLERS MARSTON MOTTE

SP 320499

The village is named after the Botelers, who held the manor from the Earls of Leicester. By a stream to the south is a platform or low motte of rectangular shape, now in a poor condition. It would have been protected by wide wet moats.

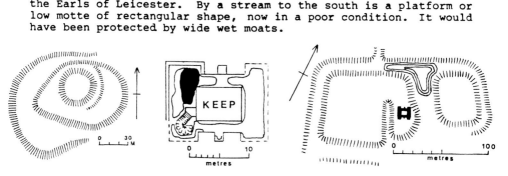

PLAN OF BRAILES CASTLE   PLANS OF BRANDON CASTLE

Brinklow Castle

CALUDON CASTLE

At the end of the 12th century the Earl of Chester granted Caludon to Stephen de Segrave, who probably built the first manor house. A park of 20 acres and a pool are recorded at Caludon in 1279 and Edward I licensed John de segrave to crenellate the manor house in 1305. On the death of John, Lord Segrave in 1353 Caludon passed to his daughter Elizabeth and her husband John de Mowbray, who are thought to have obtained another licence for crenellation in 1354. In 1385 a tiled building of four bays inside the bridge, a tiled building of seven bays outside the bridge, and a thatched barn of five bays are recorded as being in a poor state of repair. Thomas Mowbray was created Duke of Norfolk in 1397, and was residing at Caludon in 1398 when he appeared at Gosford Green for the abortive duel which Richard II had ordered him to fight with the Duke of Hereford after each had accused the other of treason. In the event the King stopped the fight before it began and banished both.

After the death of the Lady Anne Mowbray, wife of Richard, Duke of York, in 1481, the castle passed to William, Lord Berkeley, and Henry, Lord berkeley is said to have rebuilt it in the 1580s, with further additions being made by Elizabeth, Lady Berkeley in the early 17th century. In 1631 George, Lord Berkeley sold Caludon to Thomas Morgan, in whose time, or shortly after, the place was left to decay, possibly as a result of damage recieved during or after a supposed siege in the Civil War. The lands passed through the Preston and Clifford families before being broken up in 1815. Just over a century later Coventry Corporation aquired most of the land for housing, but the castle site was luckily preserved as a public recreation ground.

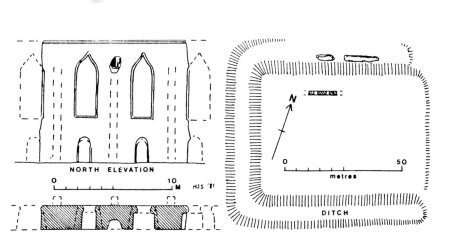

NORTH ELEVATION

DITCH

PLANS OF CALUDON CASTLE

The site now comprises a level platform 70m long by 48m wide surrounded, except on the east, where it has been filled in, by a ditch about 15m wide which is now dry. This platform may date from the time of the 1305 licence but the one fragment of masonry still standing within it about 5m away from the north side, has windows of a form which must be later, and fit much better with the date of the supposed second licence of 1354. The fragment is 2m thick and 10m high by 12.5m long and represents two complete bays, with the ends of two other bays, of the north wall of a block containing the main castle hall set over a basement. There are remains of two light windows at both levels, the hall windows having ogival heads and being large and impressive.

Caludon Castle

23

Castle Bromwich Motte

CASTLE BROMWICH MOTTE   SP 143901

This mound lies north of Castle Bromwich church overlooking the
River Tame and junction 5 on the M6. One of the feeder roads for
the latter has been cut through the site of the large bailey to
the east and south, leaving the mound curiously isolated with a
high retaining wall on its south side, while the northern side has
suffered from natural subsidence. The mound is now only about 5m
high, but would have appeared higher when the ditch separating it
from the bailey existed on the sides facing flat ground. Nothing
now remains of a monument erected on it in the 19th century by the
Bridgmans. Castle Bromwich was held in the 12th and 13th centuries
by a family of knights called de Bromwich with the Paganels and de
Someries of Dudley as their overlords.

CHESWICK GREEN MOAT   SP 130761

Excavations were carried out on this considerable earthwork before
most of it was destroyed to make way for a new housing estate. It
was discovered that the defences had been created in c1300 over a
previously unfortified site. The 6m wide wet moat is now filled in
and only part of the 6m high and 20m wide rampart now remains.

CHEYLESMORE MANOR   SP 333785

In the early 13th century the Earl of Chester abandoned Coventry
Castle, which was hemmed in by the fast growing city, and developed
a manor house at Cheylesmore to the south.   There was already an
extensive park there by the 1150s. The house probably had a moat
but was not seriously defensible, and Richard II demanded that it
was included within the section of the city walls licensed in 1385.
     From 1243 to 1329 the manor was held by the Montalts and then
went to Queen Isabel, who was often in residence until her death
in 1358. It then went to Edward the Black Prince, who also stayed
at Cheylesmore quite often. At Richard II's accession in 1377 the
manor became a royal possession, remaining so until 1549, when it
was granted to John Dudley, Earl of Warwick. It was subsequently
leased by the city council, and, after a lengthy dispute from 1661
with the Townsend family over possession, was sold to the city in
1706. The house was described as ruinous in c1538 and 1659, but was
renovated by Sir Robert Townsend in the period 1661-85. It was
later used as tenements, and parts replaced by weavers' houses.
     By 1945 just two ranges remained, built of a mixture of timber
brick and stone. One, probably a 14th century solar block standing
at one end of the former hall in the west wing, was demolished in
1955. The surviving modest wing is partly 14th century, but the
gateway through it is 16th century in its present form.

CHURCHOVER MOTTE

SP 515793

A motte lies immediately NE of Junction 1 on the M6. From at least the 1160s Churchover was held by the Waver family from the Earls of Stafford. It was later held by the Shirfords and Ireys.

COMPTON WYNIATES

SP 330418

The house lies in a dip and was formerly called Compton in the Hole. In 1205 Philip de Compton held the manor from the Earl of Warwick. The present brick mansion was begun c1500-10 by Sir William Compton. The park was formed c1513-19 and shortly afterwards the house was extended and altered using materials which Henry VIII allowed Sir William to remove from the disused castle of Fulbrook. His grandson Henry was made a baron by Elizabeth I and in 1618 James I created Henry's son William Earl of Northampton. Spencer, 2nd Earl was a Royalist casualty at the battle of Hopton Heath in 1643 and during the same year the house was occupied by Parliamentary troops. They beat off an attack by Sir Charles Compton in 1644. By the end of the conflict the nearby chapel and outbuildings had been wrecked and in the 1660s James, 3rd Earl repaired the house using materials from the latter. Spencer, 8th Earl, got into debt and lived abroad from 1768. Luckily his steward ignored instructions to demolish the house for its materials. The windows were mostly bricked up to avoid paying tax and part was later leased to a farmer. Eventually it was restored by the 3rd Marquess of Northampton and it was then that the southern and east sections of the moat were filled in.

The house has four ranges around a court 17m square. The north and west ranges are 6m wide, the south range was 7.5m wide, and the east range containing the hall was 9m wide. The porch on the west with side doorways originally to the berm between the walls and the former moat, the projecting aisled chancel of the chapel with a big end window, the lofty turreted tower beside it and the six small polygonal turrets around the north and west sides are all slightly later additions. The tower-like NW wing, thinly walled like all the rest of the house, is thought to have been built in the 1660s from older materials, and the east wing was doubled in width in a style matching the older work in the 1730s. The hall roof and perhaps the bay window may be among reused material from Fulbrook.

Compton Wyniates

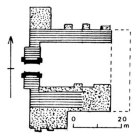

PLAN OF COUGHTON COURT

*Coughton
Court*

COUGHTON COURT   SP 084606

Coughton (pronounced Co-ton) Court lies immediately south of where
a stream flows into the western bank of the Arrow and was formerly
protected by a wet moat, now filled in, which the Spiney family may
have had dug in the 13th or 14th century. They are credited with
the building of the lowest stage of the westward facing gatehouse,
a structure 9m deep by 7.5m wide with four square corner turrets
and a fan-vaulted passage. The upper parts were added by Sir George
Throckmorton soon after he succeeded to Coughton in 1518. The half
timbered north and south ranges nearly 6m wide had been built by
his father Robert. They have been extensively remodelled, that on
the south having been widened towards the court in c1600 and on the
other side in the 1660s. The latter work formed part of extensive
repairs carried out after the Civil War for in 1643, the year in
which Charles I made Sir Robert Throckmorton a baronet, Coughton
was occupied by Parliamentary forces, and early in 1644 they were
unsuccessfully besieged by a Royalist force from Worcester. Several
of the Throckmortons were noted Catholics, Francis Throckmorton
having been executed in 1583 for plotting against Elizabeth I, and
the wives of the Gunpowder Plotters assembled at the house in 1605.
Shortly after James II went into exile in 1688 Coughton Court was
wrecked by a Protestant mob from nearby Alcester. The east range,
which presumably contained the original main hall, was not restored
and was demolished in 1780 after a new hall was made in the south
range. The house is now administered by the National Trust although
the Throckmortons still live in it.

*Swanswell
Gate,
Coventry*

COVENTRY CASTLE & CITY WALLS

At about the time of William II's accession in 1087, Coventry was given to the Earl of Chester. He or one of his early 12th century successors built a castle there. In 1143 Robert Marmion of Tamworth siezed the adjacent priory, and fortified it against the Earl, and in 1146 King Stephen ordered the castle to be surrendered to him. The Earl tried to recover the castle by force in 1147, but Stephen came to relieve it. There were several skirmishes in the neighbour-hood, during which the King was slightly wounded but succeeded in routing the Earl. The King then demolished the castle, but it was evidently rebuilt as it is referred to in charters of the reigns of Henry II and John. However, Earl Ranulph de Blundeville, d1232, seems to have abandoned the castle in favour of greater seclusion at the manor house of Cheylesmore further to the south (see page 24).

Coventry's size and importance must have caused it to have a ditch and other rudimentary defences by the late 12th century. In 1329 Edward III granted the priory and citizens a licence for the building of embattled walls around the city but work only appears to have begun in 1335, when the mayor, Richard de Stoke, laid the first stone of New Gate. Work proceeded slowly around the south and west sides throughout the later 14th century and then in the 15th the priory lands north of the Sherborne were enclosed. The work was only just finished before Leland's visit in the 1530s as the city found the construction and maintenance of the walls a considerable financial burdon. The defences were sufficient, however, to enable the city to play a part as a fortress in the struggles of the 1450s and 60s. By the early 17th century the walls were already becoming neglected but were restored by pro-Parliamentarian forces in 1642. In that year King Charles I appeared before the city and breached New Gate with cannonfire before Lord Brooke arrived and the King withdrew to the north, leaving Brooke to set up his headquarters in the city. A tower was built, and other work carried out on the walls in 1644 in readiness for a Royalist siege which never took place.

Charles II saw Coventry as a den of rebels and in 1662 sent the Earl of Northampton to demolish its walls. Only part was destroyed before there was a change of heart, the remainder being maintained in the 1670s and 80s, with several gatehouses being let as private dwellings. All twelve gates survived well into the 18th century and were only demolished when they began to hinder traffic.

The walls at Coventry were nearly three miles long, enclosing an area three quarters of a mile long by half a mile wide, which was equalled only at London and Norwich. All that survives is a ruinous length connecting the simple rectangular Cook Street Gate and Swanswell Gate, being within a park called Lady Herbert's Garden. New Gate, removed in 1762, was rectangular with a single turret, later replaced by two gables. Gosford Gate, removed in 1765, had round bartizans on the outer side and adjoined St George's chapel. Spon Gate, demolished in 1771, had two polygonal towers on the outer side, and the inner side of the lowest level extended almost to St John's church. The Greyfriars Gate was built soon after the additional licence granted in 1385, and was demolished in 1781. It was rectangular with two round towers on the outer corners. Bishop Street Gate was built by 1411, rebuilt in 1689, and taken down in 1765. It was a two storey rectangular structure. Well Street Gate, Hill Street Gate, and Bastille Gate were all similar. The latter was given an extra storey in the late 17th century, and survived until 1849, being the last of the gates to be destroyed.

Castle Yard, Fillongley

PLAN OF
CASTLE YARD,
FILLONGLEY

0   50
L_I_I_I_I_I M

FILLONGLEY CASTLE

SP 280867 & 285877

The precise historical relationship between the two castle sites at
Fillongley is unclear. The site at Castle Hills seems to have been
abandoned by Henry III's time when it was called Old Fillongley and
then or slightly later the Castle Yard site was refortified with
stone walls by the Hastings family who owed service to the Marmions
of Tamworth, who held Fillongley from Peterborough Abbey. Possibly
Castle Yard was established during Stephen's reign to rival Castle
Hills then held by Maud's supporters the Montforts. Although Henry
de Hastings was forfeited after the Battle of Evesham in 1265 his
son Sir John was restored by Edward I in 1283, created a baron in
1290, and given licence to crenellate his house at Fillongley and
hold a weekly market in the village in 1301. The last of this line
was John, Lord Hastings, d1389, after which Fillongley became part
of the Bergavenny barony held by the Beauchamps and Nevilles. They
probably left it to decay as they had numerous seats elsewhere.

Both sites lie beside streams and were protected by wet moats.
Castle Hills is a ringwork 60m by 45m, with a substantial rampart
but no outer defences apart from the moat. Castle Yard has an oval
bailey 70m by 40m with traces of a rampart on the south and on the
north several fallen fragments of a rectangular stone building.

Hartshill Castle

FULBROOK CASTLE

SP 252607

The moated site immediately west of Court Farm is thought to have been the site of the moated manor house held in 1324 by John de Hastings, Lord Bergavenny. From one of the three water filled arms which survive a globular steel yard weight with shields thought to be of mid 13th century date was recovered in 1841. A second square moated site lies close to the north. When John de Hastings, 2nd Earl of Pembroke, died in 1389 Fulbrook passed to Reynold de Grey, the house being described in 1392 as a hall with a solar and chapel adjoining with a kitchen and byre under one roof all inside a moat with a gatehouse containing a stable with a chamber above beyond the moat. In 1412 Joan, Lady Bergavenny, seems to have renovated the decayed house and to have built a 'sumptuous' new gatehouse on the site of the old one. The sandstone masonry in the lower part of the west wall of the farmhouse may be a relic of this structure.

In the 1420s Fulbrook was held by John, Duke of Bedford, who built a 'praty castle made of stone and brike' in the field called Castle Hill south of the brook and the moated sites just mentioned. It passed to Henry VI when the Duke died in 1435, and was ruinous as early as 1478 when it reverted to the Crown on the attainder of George, Duke of Clarence. Henry VIII allowed Sir William.Compton, keeper of Fulbrook Park, to demolish the buildings and use some of the materials for his new house at Compton Wyniates. Nothing stands above ground but brick lined foundations are said to have been found and bricks and tile and pottery sherds have been ploughed up.

HALFORD CASTLE

SP 260455

An enclosure and mound once lay beside where the Fosse Way crosses the River Stock. In 1332 there is a mention of a Robert de Castro and John Atte Castel, so the castle may have been in use then.

HARTSHILL CASTLE

SP 325944

Hugh de Hartshill probably erected the motte and bailey on a ridge c1135-40. Robert de Hartshill was killed fighting for Simon de Montfort at Evesham in 1265, and the castle was given to Warine de Bassingburn of Cambridgeshire, but was later restored to Robert's son John. His grandson John is said to have built the curtain wall of the bailey in Edward II's reign. After he died Hartshill passed to the Culpeppers of Kent until it was sold in c1550. The Purefoy's held the castle during the 17th century but sold it in 1702 to Sir Nathan Wright, Keeper of the Great Seal. It was sold again in 1751 and 1791 and passed through several families in the 19th century.

Old print of Hartshill Castle

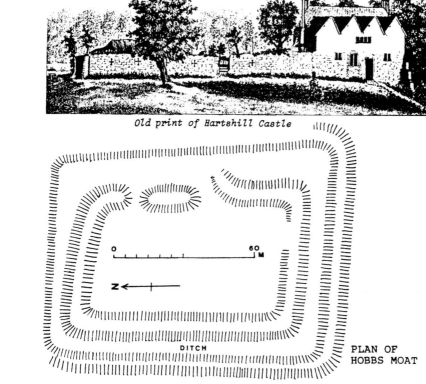

DITCH

PLAN OF
HOBBS MOAT

The very overgrown motte lies at the NW end of the site. Moats formed in the bottom of mostly natural hollows protect the NE and SW sides of the bailey which is roughly a square of 60m with the south corner chamfered off. A ruinous wall 1.2m thick pierced with crossloops at intervals of about 4.5m surrounds the bailey except on the SE side where there remains one jamb of the gateway. There are buttresses at the north and east corners but there were never any towers or turrets. In the middle of the NE side is the chapel, about 11m long by 4.8m wide with traces of a piscina. The only other internal building of substance was a late 16th century house which had four gables on the NE side. Only the SE end gable now remains, having a projecting chimney breast.

HOBBS MOAT

SP 147826

This substantial earthwork lies among trees on an eminence south of Solihull. A high rampart, rising up to 6m above the dry ditch surrounding it, encloses an area 90m long by 60m wide. The site is traditionally associated with a castle or homestead belonging to the Odinsells family. It probably dates between the end of the 12th century and the beginning of the 14th century.

ILMINGTON BATTERY

SP 200428

The slight traces of an earthwork on the hill high above Ilmington are more likely to be relics of a Civil War fort than a manorial moated site of the medieval period.

KENILWORTH CASTLE

In 1086 Kenilworth formed part of the royal manor of Stoneleigh but in 1120 Henry I gave it to his chamberlain Geoffrey de Clinton. The latter used the southern part of the estate to found an Augustinian priory and the northern part for a motte and bailey castle provided with an adjoining lake made by building a dam across the valley, and having a park beyond. During the rebellion of his sons in 1173 Henry II took over the castle and garrisoned it with 160 men. The King had no other castle of note in Warwickshire and seems to have been keen to retain it so an exchange of lands was eventually made, perhaps in 1182, with Henry de Clinton. There is a record of royal expenditure on it in 1184. Probably the keep and inner bailey walls were under construction throughout the 1180s. When Richard I became King in 1189 he had the castle put into a defensible state before going off crusading. His successor John visited Kenilworth several times between 1204 and 1215, and, mostly in the period 1210-15, spent large sums on making it impregnable with the addition of the outer wall and the raising of the dam with the consequent enlargement of the lake. Kenilworth was one of the four royal castles required to be surrendered to the barons as a surety for the king keeping to the terms of Magna Carta, but as John still had a garrison there in 1216 it seems that the castle was never actually handed over.

Henry III spent minor sums on the castle but used it little. By 1241 the great chamber was roofless, the keep forebuilding was ruined, part of the outer wall was leaning outwards towards the lake, and repairs were needed to the two gates and the chapel. The castle was handed over to the King's sister Eleanor, who in 1238 married Simon de Montfort, created Earl of Leicester in 1239. They probably built the Water Tower and the enclosure called The Brays defending the southern end of the dam during the 1250s. Simon was compelled to surrender Kenilworth under the terms of the Provisions of Oxford laid down by Parliament in 1258 forbidding foreigners to hold royal castles, but he recovered it in 1254 when he led many of the barons against Henry and captured him in battle at Lewes. The castle held Prince Edward as a hostage for his father's behaviour at the end of the year. The Prince escaped in 1265 and managed to surprise a force led by the Earl's son Simon which was encamped by the castle. In fact Simon the Younger only escaped being captured by swimming the moat in his nightshirt. Soon afterwards the royal army defeated and killed the Earl at Evesham. In November Simon the Younger left the castle and ordered the garrison to surrender but they feared the King's wrath and refused. In the end they held out until surrendering on honourable terms in December 1266.

Kenilworth Castle: General view from the dam

*Great Hall
undercroft,
Kenilworth
Castle*

The siege of Kenilworth personally directed by King Henry and Prince Edward throughout the second half of 1266 is one of the most celebrated of sieges in medieval England and demonstrates just how effective broad expanses of water could be for defending a large and well stocked fortress held by a resolute garrison. Mining or scaling the walls was impossible. The garrison used stone throwing engines to good effect and shattered the belfreys or wooden towers with which the royal forces attempted to command the walls. Barges were brought from Chester for an unsuccessful attack across the mere. When the Archbishop of Canterbury excommunicated the garrison one of them appeared on the battlements dressed in a white shirt and in turn excommunicated the Archbishop. Eventually, in October terms were offered and it was agreed that the castle would be given up if not relieved in 40 days. At the end the garrison technically were undefeated militarily and were allowed to march out into exile keeping their arms and armour.

After the siege Henry gave Kenilworth to his younger son Edmund, Earl of Lancaster. In 1279 Roger Mortimer organised at the castle a Round table or tournament attended by 100 knights who tilted on the summit of the dam. The next Earl, Thomas, who succeeded in 1299, began a collegiate chapel in the outer ward but his plans were left incomplete when he was executed and attainted for rebellion against Edward II. In 1326 the castle was the scene of the King's enforced acceptance of being deposed from the throne, and it was restored to Thomas's brother Henry. His son Henry, who succeeded in 1345, was created Duke of Lancaster. He had the hall re-roofed in 1347.

Edward III's third son John of Gaunt married Blanche, daughter of Duke Henry, and was in turn created Duke of Lancaster. He held Kenilworth from 1361 to 1399 and during the 1380s reconstructed the hall and private apartments to form a palacial suite the equal of anything then standing in Britain. His son became Henry IV in 1399 and his grandson Henry V laid out a moated summer house with timber buildings and a harbour at the north end of the lake in 1414. In 1456 Henry VI sent 30 cannon and other stores to the castle during his struggles with Richard, Duke of York. The next alterations date from the 1520s when Henry VIII had a half timbered range built on the east side of the inner ward and the buildings of the Plesaunce or summer house were re-erected against the crosswall dividing the outer ward on the west side below John of Gaunt's Great Hall.

Lunn's Tower, stables, and chapel foundations, Kenilworth Castle

The castle was granted to John Dudley, Duke of Northumberland, in 1553 but reverted to the Crown after Queen Mary executed him for trying to put Lady Jane Grey on the throne. However, his son Robert became a favourite of Queen Elizabeth and she granted Kenilworth and many other estates to him in 1563, making him Earl of Leicester in 1564. He entertained the Queen at the castle three times and on the last occasion, in July 1575, she stayed for 18 days of hunting, dancing, allegorical presentations, and other amusements. The Earl in preparation for these visits added a tall block of apartments at the SE corner of the inner ward, remodelled the keep, built a new northward facing gatehouse and a long stable block on the east side of the outer ward, and filled in much of the northern moat. A formal garden was also laid out on the north side of the outer ward.

Shortly after James I's accession in 1603 the castle reverted to the Crown and a survey extolls the virtues of the accommodation available within it which was regarded as adequate for simultaneous visits by the King, Queen, and Prince Henry. However, Leicester's alterations had reduced its value as a fortress and in 1642 Charles I withdrew his garrison and the castle was occupied by Parliamentary troops. In September 1649 Sir William Dugdale made drawings of the castle which were published in his Antiquities of Warwickshire of 1656. An order for the slighting of the castle made before Dugdale's visit was carried out shortly afterwards, the north walls of the keep and outer bailey being demolished. The breaching of the dams to drain the mere and convert it to pasture was carried out either then or shortly afterwards by Colonel Hawksworthe, who purchased the estate for £2,000 and converted Leicester's gatehouse into his residence. In Charles II's reign Kenilworth was held by the Hyde Earls of Rochester for two generations, and then was granted to Thomas Villiers, created Earl of Clarendon. His descendants held it until it was purchased in 1937 and handed over to the Ministry of Works for preservation as a national monument. It had become a popular tourist attraction as a result of Sir Walter Scott's novel 'Kenilworth' first published in 1821 in which a plan was given and Elizabeth I's visit in 1575 fictionally described in detail.

Leicester's Gatehouse, Kenilworth　　　　　*Lunn's Tower, Kenilworth*

In the 1970s the dam was partly restored and visitors now use the original medieval approach, parking their cars in the court called The Brays which defended the south end of the dam, and then walking across the dam to Mortimer's Tower. The Brays measures 180m by 80m and has a bank with various projections, the foundations of a twin towered gate, and a ditch which was formerly filled with water held back by a dam on the north side of the present access road. The tiltyard enclosed by thin 13th century walls on the dam is 15m wide by 110m long. In front of the ruined 12th century Gallery tower at the south end is a small 13th century barbican in front of which was a drawbridge.

Roger Mortimer, who presided over the tournament of 1279, gave his name to the main gatehouse of the outer ward. Originally just a simple rectangular tower of c1185, later, perhaps in the 1230s, twin round fronted towers were added in front. The passage between them was closed with a portcullis and a pair of doors. Behind the western tower is a latrine projection beside the older tower wall. The outer ward had a secondary entrance in the middle of the north wall which was entirely destroyed in c1650. At its extremities the wall was flanked by two towers of c1210-5. The Swan Tower has an octagonal upper storey, now very ruined, set on a square base, and the round Lunn's Tower, 10m in diameter, has pilaster buttresses which are pierced by crossloops with triangular feet rising from a broad base, and also a stair in a polygonal turret giving access to two upper storeys. The Water Tower is a fine structure of the 1250s which is polygonal above a square base towards the field and has two fine rooms connected by a spiral stair. The upper room has well preserved two light windows in embrasures with seats. Nearby, the curtain to the SW is widened to contain a remarkable mural chamber with a fireplace and a short passage to a latrine. No towers lie along the west and south sections of the outer wall which were well protected by the mere. Stability of the wall has been a problem here and there are many buttresses, most of them contemporary with the sections of wall they adjoin. Several sections were rebuilt during the 14th century, there are four short sections of modern patching, and the part on the south which is thicker than the rest may be a rebuilding of c1250. The original thickness was mostly about 1.6m but the vulnerable north wall was somewhat more massive than that.

34

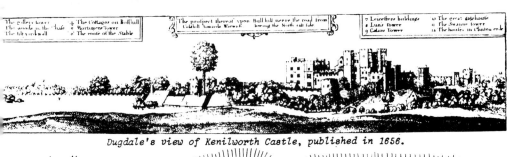

Dugdale's view of Kenilworth Castle, published in 1656.

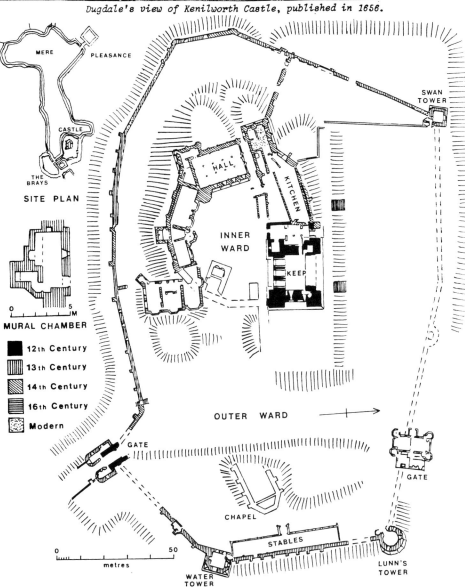

PLANS OF KENILWORTH CASTLE

35

The Keep
Forebuilding,

Leicester's Buildings & Gaunt's Tower
Kenilworth Castle

Leicester's gatehouse was built to provide easier access to the church, village, and park. It is a three storey block 15m long by 7m wide with four corner turrets and mullion and transom windows. The porch on the west side has material thought to have come from Leicester's block by the inner ward, whilst the wing of two storeys and an attic on the west was added in the 1650s when the passage was blocked up and the building made into a private residence which it still remains. The contemporary stable block 44m long built beside the east curtain of the outer ward has a stone lower stage with the upper walls half timbered and also remains roofed, being used for a cafe and displays. West of it are the footings of the early 14th century collegiate church with a polygonal east end.

The keep, labelled by Dugdale as Caesar's Tower, is one of the largest and most massive medieval towers in Britain. It measures 24.2m by 17.8m over walls more than 4m thick which are externally stepped out for another 4m to form a massive base said to engulf the original motte, although some claim that there is a filled-in vaulted basement below the present lowest level high above that of the inner ward. At each corner are towers varying slightly in size but averaging 8m by 7m. They project as much as 3.3m from the main wall faces which have two intermediate pilasters on the long sides and one on the end walls. The NW tower contained latrines and the NW tower has a wide spiral stair which connected the two principal rooms. The southern towers originally contained chambers only at the upper storey level but the base of the SW tower was hollowed out to provide chambers in the 1570s when the adjacent forebuilding was remodelled and the original narrow windows with round arched embrasures splayed and stepped both internally and externally were cut away for the insertion of mullion and transom windows. In the east wall one of the original windows survives, with a well shaft beside it which is accessible at both levels. The forebuilding originally contained steps up to the entrance at the upper level. The wall gallery above roof level has crossloops with triangular bases like those on Lunn's Tower, so this part and the battlements, now lost, must have been King John's work. Probably the keep was unfinished at Henry II's death in 1189 and Richard simply left it.

Little remains of the original wall of the inner ward because of later refacing and rebuilding. The fragment against the keep has one jamb of the entrance with a portcullis groove and suggests it was up to 3m thick and 10m high. Henry VIII's block lay south of this gate but has vanished, although there are foundations of the 13th century chapel. Beyond, at the SE corner, is the fine block built by the Earl of Leicester in 1570. It has three bay windows facing east, foundations of one facing north, and a diagonally projecting SW wing which seems to have contained a staircase above a solid base. The southern part of the building has a basement over which were three storeys each containing a self contained suite of rooms suitable for the Queen and others of high rank. The northern room of each level extended further west than the other rooms and was a large audience chamber. The middle section contained a small audience chamber reached by a passage wainscoted off from a service room to the west which had access to a waste chute, and the south room was the bedchamber.

On the north side of the inner ward is the kitchen, now very ruined. It was 8m wide by as much as 23m long and is basically of the 1380s, although the ovens at the eastern end are 15th century. from the west end a service stair leads up to a lobby in the Strong Tower, one of two wings with octagonal corner turrets which project westwards at each end of the hall as part of the remodelling of the 1380s. The tower has rib-vaults at each level, hence its name, and above hall level contained a suite for a household official. The main access to the hall for visitors was via a stair leading up to a vaulted porch. There was a court between the stair and kitchen. The hall was one of the largest and finest secular apartments of medieval Britain, being 27.6m long by 14m wide. It was divided into six bays with lofty transomed two-light windows in huge embrasures with seats in the second, third, and fifth bays from north to south. The first bay was probably screened off as a passage with a gallery for musicians above, the fourth bay has fireplaces, and the sixth bay opened onto an oriel on the east towards the court, and onto chambers in the SW wing, which Dugdale called the Saintlowe Tower. The bays are divided externally by buttresses which on the west take an unusual triangular form; internally there were divided by the roof trusses, which seem to have been of the hammer-beam type. Below the hall was an undercroft of the same size, vaulted in a pattern of six by three bays with rows of piers. A thin crosswall divided off a passage leading to a postern at the northern end.

From the Saintlowe Tower there was access to the main audience room, called the White Chamber. It was 16m long by 7m wide and had a floor supported on wooden piers in the cellar below. It had an original bay window towards the field and two bay windows of 1570 towards the court. East of it was a lesser audience chamber reached by a spiral stair from the court adjoining an octagonal vaulted porch. Between the two chambers was an irregularly shaped service room, off which open latrines in Gaunt's Tower, which is polygonal towards the field. The tower contained bedrooms at a higher level.

KENTS MOAT   SP 144863

This site may have been where the de Sheldon family resided in the 13th century. The de Paytos seem to have had a house here in the period 1347-73 and apparently carried out some building work, but Sir Hugh and Sir Ralph Shirley held it in the early 15th century. However there was no resident lord of the manor after 1440, and by the late 18th century all memory of buildings here were forgotten. The site was excavated in 1964 before the rampart inside the ditch was levelled and blocks of flats were built inside the enclosure.

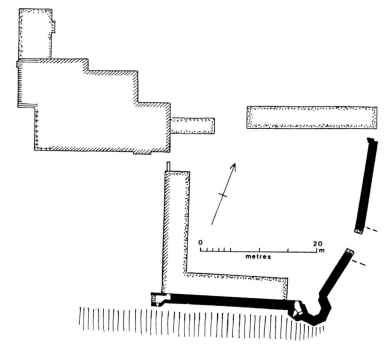

PLAN OF KINGSBURY HALL

KINETON CASTLE

SP 330508

On a slight rise west of the village are the very overgrown remains of a motte now only about 2m high with faint traces of a D-shaped bailey 60m by 40m to the north. The position is almost surrounded by streams which could have provided extensive water defences. The castle is sometimes named after King John who was granted Kineton (or Kington) by Richard I in 1198, though it is probably older than his time. John granted it to Stephen de Seagrave in 1216 and later it passed to the Mowbrays.

KINGSBURY HALL

SP 214964

The de Bracebridge family held Kingsbury in the 13th century. They fortified the hall in the 14th century, and sold it to Sir Francis Willoughby in 1585. When Sir Henry Willoughby died in 1649 it went to his daughter Anne who married Sir Thomas Aston of Cheshire. The hall lies north of the church overlooking a steep drop to the Tame. A thin crosswall divides a platform about 60m by 36m into east and west courts. The west court has strong natural defences and has in the NW corner a house of c1500 which has been remodelled several times. The west end of the main block is 18th century and the west extension of the NW wing is of c1590. Modern farm buildings line three sides of the east court. To the east and south it has a 14th century curtain wall 1.6m thick and 6m high. It has a rebuilt arch on the east which formerly had a gatehouse 7.5m wide in front and a small polygonal tower with a latrine in a western projection lies at the SE corner. The curtain is broken off at the site of another latrine by the crosswall. There is a deep ditch to the south and to the east was a wet moat probably once crossed by a drawbridge.

Kingsbury Hall

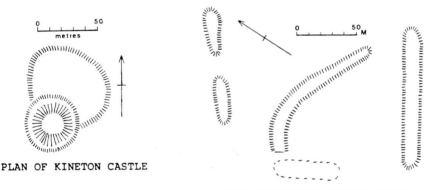

PLAN OF KINETON CASTLE

PLAN OF LANGLEY CASTLE SITE

LANGLEY CASTLE
SP 152956

The de Bereford family held Langley in the 13th century under the overlordship of the Earls of Warwick. In 1327 Edward III licenced his clerk Edmund de Bereford to crenellate his house at Langley. Edmund's father William, d1325, was one of those who complained to Edward II of the extortion and violence of John de Somery, Lord of Dudley, and fortifying the house must have seemed a necessity in the prevailing atmosphere of lawlessness. Langley later passed to the Hores and then the Pudseys. In the late 17th century it passed by marriage to the Jessons, and then to the Pearsons and Lynches. Traces of footings of possible 14th century stonework and slight remains of later brick walls were visible early in the 20th century but by the 1980s all that remained were two tree covered hollows marking the line of two sections of the moat. Another side of the moat was filled in early in this century. By the site is a newly renovated stable block of much later date, now used as housing.

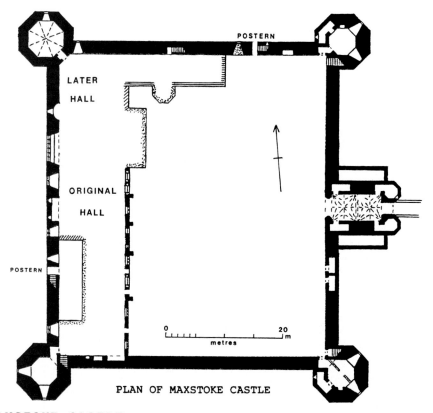

POSTERN

LATER
HALL

ORIGINAL
HALL

POSTERN

0   20
metres   m

PLAN OF MAXSTOKE CASTLE

MAXSTOKE CASTLE

SP 224892

When Edmund Odingseles died shortly after his father William in
1295 Maxstoke passed to his eldest sister Ida who married John de
Clinton, d1310. In the 1330s the manor was effectively divided in
two when their younger son William, Earl of Huntingdon, built the
Augustinian priory in the southern part. Subsequently he erected
the castle in the northern part as a residence for his heir John,
his elder brother's son. According to Dugdale, Earl William, d1354,
obtained a licence to crenellate the castle from Edward III in 1346.

John, Lord Clinton and Say, exchanged Maxstoke with Humphrey,
6th Earl of Stafford for two manors in Northamptonshire. Humphrey,
created Duke of Buckingham in 1444, remodelled the apartments at
the castle. He was killed in 1459 at the battle of Northampton,
his grandson and heir Henry, 2nd Duke, was executed by Richard III
in 1483, and Henry's son Edward, restored to the honours and title
as 3rd Duke by Henry VII in 1485, was executed and attainted for
treason by Henry VIII in 1521. The estates were then surveyed and
it was reported that although Maxstoke Castle was decayed the sum
of £100 would have seen it repaired as a fit place for the King
and Queen to stay in when progressing around the country.

However, towards the end of 1521, Henry VIII granted Maxstoke
to Sir William Compton. His grandson Henry, born after his father's
death in 1544, was created Lord Compton. In 1597 William, 2nd Lord
Compton, conveyed Maxstoke to Sir Thomas Egerton, from whom in 1599
the castle passed to Thomas Dilke. It continued to descend in the
male line of the Dilke family until the last of them died in 1918,
when his nephew assumed the Dilke name, arms, and honours.

Maxstoke Castle

Lord Brooke installed a garrison of 50 men in the castle in February 1643 and they continued to hold it for Parliament until November 1648. Although the Council of State then considered having the fortifications slighted they have remained intact until the present day. In 1745 part of the Duke of Cumberland's army was billetted in barns and outbuildings of the castle when he was on his way north towards Derby to fight Bonny Prince Charlie.

The castle has a single rectangular court 51m by 46m with a curtain wall about 2m thick beyond which is a wet moat. At each corner is an octagonal tower 9m in diameter and 13m high to the top of the parapet, which like that on the curtain has no shooting slits. Three of the towers contain three storeys of lodgings for retainers with latrines, tiny fireplaces, and windows of one or two ogee headed lights. The thinner walled NW tower contains three upper storeys which probably opened off the original lord's suite, and a vaulted basement which served as a strongroom. In the middle of the east side is a boldly projecting gatehouse with octagonal turrets facing the field. The main block has two upper rooms over a passage with a two bay tierceron vault with large bosses. The doors have remains of iron sheeting with a honeysuckle pattern and the Stafford badge. A shield on the east parapet has the Clinton arms.

The castle originally has an 11m wide range containing a great hall on the west side, and 9m wide north and south ranges. There is no evidence of an east range although there are two latrines south of the gatehouse in the curtain wall. The north and south ranges did not last long although fireplaces and windows serving the rooms remain in the curtain walls. The ranges vanished before or during a remodelling of the west range in the late 15th century when a new hall was created in the NW corner. The tall hall windows and the huge six-light chapel window piercing the west curtain wall seem to belong to an earlier remodelling, probably of the 1390s. The eastern wall of the original hall remains but this chamber, and the chapel, both set over basements, have been subdivided and much remodelled at various periods, particularly in the 1820s when a new projection containing the entrance and stair was added. East of the later hall is a narrow three storey early 16th century half timbered range. On the second storey is a large chamber with two large windows through the curtain wall. Between is a fireplace with an oak overmantle of c1600 with the arms of Sir Thomas Dilke and his wife Anne Fisher.

41

MORTON BAGOT CASTLE

South of the church is an eye-shaped enclosure 57m by 37m probably best interpreted as a 12th century ringwork. The enclosure is not level and there is a pool to the east at a lower level than the bottom of the dry western ditch.

MOUNTGREVELL HALL

William Grevill of Chipping Campden obtained the manor of Milcote in I401. Queen Elizabeth I in 1567 granted Ludovic Grevill licence to rebuild the manor house, embattle it, and call it Mountgrevell. The house was begun but never completed and nothing remains of it. Ludovic got into financial difficulties probably as a result of the cost of the building so he had two of his servants murder Richard Webb of Drayton in Oxfordshire and then obtained the latter's lands by means of a forged will. Ludovic died under torture in 1589 after being arrested for murdering one of the servants when the latter seemed about to give away his guilty secret. The manor was conveyed to Lord Cranfield in 1622 and later went to the Earls of Dorset.

NEW HALL

SP 133949

The house, now a hotel, takes much of its character from the works carried out in 1870. However the hall range and the dining room to the east of it in the SE corner of the well preserved wet moat have grey medieval masonry perhaps dating back to the time of the de Sutton family. The house went to Sir John Lizours of Fledborough in Nottinghamshire in 1340, and then passed to the Bassets. In 1428 they conveyed it to Sir Richard Stanhope. The sandstone north range was probably built by Thomas Gibbons who is said to have purchased New Hall in 1552. His heirs conveyed it to Henry Sacheverell in 1610, and when his grandson George died in 1715 it passed to the Chadwicks who erected the towers on the south and west fronts which are dated 1796.

NORTHBROOK MOAT

SP 242614

SW of the modern house is the dry shallow remnant of the SW corner of the moat of the manor house of the Grants, noted Catholics in Elizabeth I's reign. She had the house searched in 1583 after the discovery of a plot against her by John Somerville, a close relative of Edward Grant and his wife Anne. Their grandson John was executed by James I for his part in the Gunpowder Plot of 1605. The sheriff then discovered Mass books and ornaments, a chalice, and a cope in a nearby pool and 'a payre of manackles for a man's necke' in the moat. The house is thought to have been dismantled soon afterwards. It was rebuilt later and was held by William Bolding in the 1660s, when it was taxed on four hearths. It in turn was later demolished.

OVERSLEY CASTLE

SP 095553

Ralph le Boteler, one of the Earl of Leicester's officials, built a castle here and it was his descendants' principal seat until they transferred to Shropshire in the 13th century. It was sold in 1550 to Sir Anthony Cook and leased to Michael and Edmund Parker who built a new house. Dugdale saw ruins on the site. It seems that the original timber buildings, later replaced in stone, were erected on the bare hilltop without any earthworks being constructed first.

Seckington Motte

POOLEY HALL
SK 258028

Pooley overlooks the west side of the Anker opposite Polesworth. It passed from the Herthills to the Cockaynes in the early 15th century and was rebuilt by Sir Thomas Cockayne c1509 with two brick ranges, one of them three storeys high, overlooking the river, and a moat, presumably, on the other sides. Pooley was conveyed to the Jennens family in the late 17th century who made various alterations.

RAGLEY CASTLE
SP 072555

In 1370 John Rous of Ragley enlarged his estate there by exchanging lands with Evesham Abbey. In 1381 he was licenced to crenellate his house and pardoned for crenellating the gatehouse without licence. When Thomas Rous died in 1523 Ragley went to his daughter Margaret, married to John Brome of Halton. Their grandson George sold Ragley and Pophills to Sir John Conway in 1591. A new house was built for the 2nd Earl of Conway on the site in the 1680s and was embellished by the Earl of Hertford in the mid and late 18th century.

RATLEY CASTLE
SP 381473

Hugh de Arden is thought to have built this small castle in c1140. It was excavated in 1968-73 and the motte was shown to have been raised over a small ringwork part of which survives as a modest court to the north. Footings of a stone gate tower were found. To the south is a larger enclosure. The site lies on a ridge west of the village. The castle was disused by the 13th century.

RUGBY CASTLE

Earthworks of a castle at Rugby were reported by Dugdale and were still visible earlier this century, but nothing remains now.

SECKINGTON CASTLE
SK 258075

This is a fine motte and bailey castle probably of c1140. The motte rises 9m to a summit 15m across. The bailey is a crescent up to 30m wide around the south and east with an entrance gap in the rampart and ditch on the SE. In c1170 Richard Bruton, who held Seckington from the Earl of Leicester, sold it to William de Campville.

STUDLEY CASTLE

SP 082638

Studley was long held by the family of the same name descended from William Corbucion. Part of the moat around a round enclosure lies north of the church. The present house within was built early in the 16th century by Thomas Atwood and was then called Corpsons.

SYDENHAMS MOAT

SP 145757

Tipping from the 1940s onwards almost filled in the moat by 1972, when excavations were begun. The platform measured 29m by 27m and was surrounded by a wet moat 15m wide by 3m deep. It may have been built by Simon de Mancette in the early 13th century, and was sold to Sir John Dean in 1304. From 1348 until the early 17th century the manor of Monkspath in which it lies was a Montford possession, but the site was not occupied after c1400.

TILEHOUSE GREEN MOAT

SP 167769

A quadrangular platform measuring 45m by 25m enclosed by a moat 18m wide was examined before a housing estate was built on it in 1983, but nothing of much interest was discovered.

WARWICK CASTLE

SP 284646

Warwick was one of several castles built by William I in 1068 to control the Midlands. It encroached on the town four houses which belonged to the Abbot of Coventry being destroyed probably not for the castle buildings themselves but to clear a field of fire along the north side. Henry, son of Robert de Beaumont, was installed as constable. William II made his Earl of Warwick in 1088 in gratitude for support in the rebellion of that year and henceforth the castle was regarded as the private property of the Earl. Henry founded a church of All Saints in the castle but Simon, Bishop of Worcester regarded its position as unsuitable and removed it c1127. Henry's son Roger, a supporter of King Stephen, is said to have died from chagrin in 1153 after the garrison at Warwick was tricked and gave up the castle to Henry of Anjou, crowned Henry II the next year.

During the revolt of Henry II's sons in 1173 the sheriff of the county remodelled the timber buildings on the motte, provisioned it with a store of wheat, and provided a guard of levies. Rebuilding in stone of the bailey walls probably followed soon afterwards as the repairs of 1191 which cost the sheriff 45s required the service of a mason named Ralph. King John bore the cost of a guard at the castle for much of 1205. During Richard Marshal's revolt of 1233 Thomas, 6th Earl, was obliged to surrender the castle to Henry III's officials as he had no male heir to offer as a hostage instead. He died in 1242 and was succeeded by his sister Margery, then married to John Marshal. He died the same year, and, being regarded as of both strength and strategic importance, the castle was administered by the Crown until she married John de Plessis shortly afterwards. He died without issue in 1263, and his wife ten years earlier, and the castle and Earldom passed to her cousin William Mauduit. In 1264, John Giffard, left in command of Kenilworth Castle by Simon de Montfort, captured Warwick Castle in a surprise attack. The wall was breached, probably on the east side, and the Earl carried off to Kenilworth to be eventually ransomed for 1,900 marks. He died childless in 1268 and was succeeded by his nephew William Beauchamp of Elmley Castle in Worcestershire.

In all there were six Beauchamp Earls of Warwick most of whom took a major part in the political events of their day. The second Earl, Guy, who succeeded in 1298 and died in 1315, brought Edward II's favourite Gaveston to Warwick in 1312, and had him executed on Blacklowe Hill. His son Thomas, only two years old in 1315, was a founder member of Edward III's new Order of The Garter and went with the King on his campaigns in france. He most probably started work on a new suite of apartments in the 1340s, and then began to replace the NE side of the castle, giving it a central gatehouse, before his death in 1367. Ransoms from high ranking prisoners taken at Poitiers in 1356 are said to have paid for the work which then continued under his son Thomas. According to a lost bailiff's ledger cited by Dugdale Guy's Tower was completed in 1394 having presumably taken at least a decade to build, and, being similar in layout and detail, Caesar's Tower cannot be much earlier, say c1370-85. Thomas was a Governor to richard II during his minority. He was one of the Lords Appellant who executed the King's unpopular favourites in 1388 and was a prisoner in the Tower of London from 1397 until Richard was deposed by Henry IV in 1399. Richard, the 5th Earl, was a hero of the French wars under Henry V and was additionally created Earl of Aumale. He has a magnificent tomb in the family chapel adjoining Warwick parish church. His son Henry was made Duke of Warwick by Henry VI but died the next year (1446) aged just 21.

When Duke Henry's infant daughter died in 1449 the heir was his sister Anne, whose husband Richard Neville, heir of the Earl of Salisbury, was confirmed as Earl of Warwick the same year. He was the famous Warwick the Kingmaker, attainted by Henry VI in 1459 for supporting the Duke of York, but restored after his cousin, York's son, was crowned Edward IV in 1461. Warwick was put out by Edward's choice of Queen in Elizabeth Woodville and the advancement of her relatives to many offices and titles, and by 1469 he had rebelled and restored Henry VI to power, Edward being captured and briefly kept at Warwick Castle. However Warwick soon fell out with some of his allies and Edward in turn was restored after Warwick and his brother were killed at the Battle of Barnet in 1471. Edward granted the castle and earldom to his own brother George, Duke of Clarence. In 1478 Clarence was executed and attainted for treason. He left an infant son who was styled Earl of Warwick although he never enjoyed the estates as Henry VII regarded him as a dangerous rival, keeping him a prisoner from 1485 until he finally executed him in 1499.

Gatehouse & Caesar's Tower, Warwick

Warwick Castle from the River Avon

In 1480 it was reported to Edward IV and his council that the walls of the castle were in need of repair. Probably this meant the then still surviving wall of c1180 on the north side of the bailey. Shortly after he seized power in 1483 Richard III began to improve the defences on that side by erecting a huge rectangular tower with octagonal corner turrets furnished with gunports. Although left unfinished at his defeat and death in 1485 it seems that Henry VII saw fit to provide the tower with guns since the office of keeper of artillery at the castle was created in 1486.

The royal administration of the castle begun in 1478 continued until John Dudley was created Earl of Warwick in 1547 and Warwick Castle was handed over to him. Both then and at the time of John Leland's visit about ten years earlier the castle was recorded as decayed. The shell keep on the motte was falling down and as many as 500 cartloads of stone from the Black Friars had to be utilised to underpin the main south wall and stop the domestic buildings falling into the river. A tiled roof from the friary was reserved for re-use on a kitchen erected in the 1530s at the east end of the domestic range. Other minor repairs were carried out by the Crown in 1557, as Dudley, created Duke of Northumberland, was attainted and executed by Queen Mary in 1553.

Elizabeth I restored Ambrose Dudley to the Earldom in 1558, although the castle was not handed over until 1562. The Queen came to stay at the castle in 1566 and again in 1572, when a new range, timber framed on a stone basement, was erected especially for her at the SW end of the apartments. The accommodation was evidently well below that available now as the Earl had to move out to the Priory to leave room for all the Queen's household. The castle was returned to the Crown in 1590 when the Earl died heirless and was then reported to be very decayed, mostly as a result of lead being stolen from several of the roofs.

Sir Fulke Greville of Beauchamps' Court, a descendant of the Powick branch of the Beauchamps, custodian of the castle since 1600, was granted it outright by James I in 1604. Sir Fulke is said to have spent more than £20,000 on renovating the domestic apartments and laying out the grounds. For more than a decade his household lived at Wedgenock whilst work continued on the new apartments. He was created Baron Brooke of Beauchamps' Court in 1621 with special remainder to his cousin and adopted heir Robert who succeeded in 1628. He was killed leading a Parliamentary storming force against Lichfield Cathedral Close in 1643. The castle was put into a state of defence during the first half of 1642, earthen bulwarks being made and guns procured, and the garrison under Sir Edward Peyto of Chesterton held out when the Earl of Northampton besieged it for a fortnight in August. Northampton lacked adequate artillery for a serious bombardment and retreated when the Earl of Essex approached. In 1645 the garrison numbered more than 300 men and there were cannon mounted on the motte and perhaps also on Guy's Tower. Considerable repairs and remodelling were carried out by the 4th Lord Brooke in the 1660s and 70s. The block outside the NE curtain was added then. The 8th Lord was created Earl Brooke in 1746, and Earl of Warwick in 1759, thus re-uniting the castle and Earldom which had separate holders for several generations. He gothicised many of the windows in the apartments, refurnished some of them, and added the dining room. In 1978 the then Lord Brooke sold the castle and remaining furnishings to Madame Tussauds. They maintain the castle as one of Britain's foremost tourist attractions.

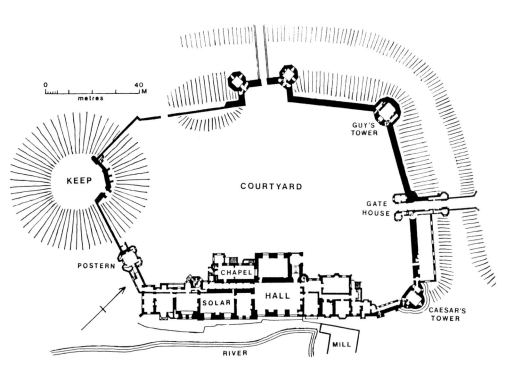

PLAN OF WARWICK CASTLE

47

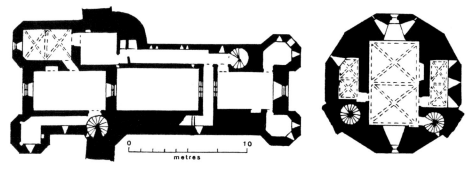

PLAN OF THE GATEHOUSE AT SECOND STOREY LEVEL   PLAN OF GUY'S TOWER

Warwick Castle is often described as the finest medieval castle in England. Certainly it is well preserved, large, has fine grounds and is splendidly situated on a shelf about 18m above the Avon, but less of the building is medieval than the casual visitor might be led to think. In fact neighbouring Kenilworth has a greater volume of medieval masonry remaining. At Warwick most of the keep has gone, little remains of the original domestic apartments other than the undercrofts, and even the parapets on the walls and towers have mostly been rebuilt. These parapets have cross-loops with roundels at the extremities, a type common in the 14th century. On a closer inspection most of the loops are renewed or are imitations of older originals. Most have the two sections of the horizontal slot not connected to the vertical slot, a vertical fillet having been left for greater strength. No medieval mason would do such a thing. Even the instruments of torture in Caesar's Tower are all post medieval.

The castle is roughly a rectangle of 120m by 85m with a steep drop to the river on the SW, an 18m high mound with later terraces on the SW, and a high curtain wall 2.5m thick around the NW and NE sides where there is a dry moat up to 25m wide. Only the three sides which faced the bailey now remain of a shell keep probably built c1230-50 with perhaps ten sides originally. The remaining sides were given a new parapet facing the mound summit in 1642 but the present cross-looped parapet was evidently not constructed hastily then and must belong to the mid 18th century like the two polygonal turrets and the buttresses. A thin 18th century wall runs eastward to the Watergate Tower which has a 14th century base with a passage closed by a portcullis, and square rooms above with staircases and closets contained in the polygonal corners.

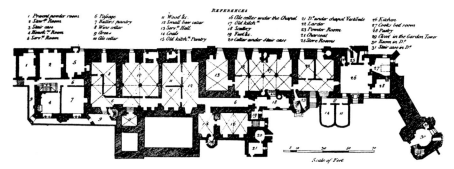

OLD PLAN OF THE CELLARS BELOW THE APARTMENTS AT WARWICK CASTLE

48

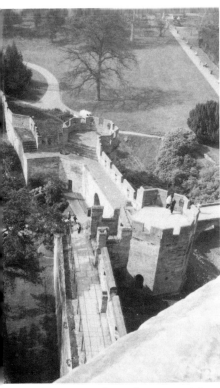

Richard III Tower from above, Warwick

Watergate
Tower,
Warwick

The apartments along the SE side of the bailey have a complex architectural history. The rib-vaulted undercrofts are all thought to be mid 14th century except for those of the 16th century at the south end which support 17th century rooms thought to lie upon the site of the timber framed lodgings built to accommodate Elizabeth I in 1572. The great hall 19m long by 11m wide was mostly rebuilt in 1871 after a fire except for two original service doorways at the NE end. The block beyond containing the library is also partly of 1871, but mostly of the 17th and 18th centuries. Running in line SW of the hall are the Green Drawing Room, Cedar Room, and Red Drawing Room which must correspond to an ante chamber, audience chamber, and private room of the 14th century layout although some consider that the Cedar Room lies on the site of a still older great hall. The Spy Tower facing the court is probably early 16th century but remodelled in the 18th. A passage divides the Cedar Room from the chapel, a 16th century room with modern windows upon a 14th century basement. The original chapel was re-roofed in 1395 as part of the preparations for a visit by Richard II. The porch and dining room beside the great hall are of 1764-6 although there was an earlier and shorter porch here. Engravings and paintings show a sequence of new windows being inserted in the river front during the mid 18th century and later. Many of the present windows are 19th century.

49

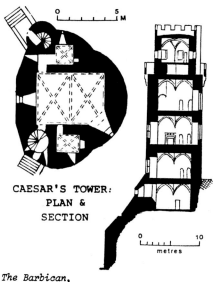

CAESAR'S TOWER:
PLAN &
SECTION

The Barbican,
Warwick Castle

Caesar's Tower is a tri-lobed structure 11m by 9.3m rising 20m to the summit of the machicolated parapet within which is a narrower section rising another 6m, but it has a massive base extending down towards the river and on that side rises no less than 44m. Below courtyard level the base contains a prison with a latrine but no other comforts and little light. At courtyard level and the next two stages are suites for household officials with a rectangular main room having one or two windows and a fireplace plus a latrine on one side and a tiny bedchamber on the other. At parapet level is a munitions store and above that a guard room. Except for the stores all six storeys are rib-vaulted, which greatly increases the structural strength of the tower. Guy's Tower is 38m high and also has a machicolated parapet. In plan it is twelve sided and about 11.5m in diameter. It has four storeys of vaulted lodging suites similar in layout to those in Caesar's Tower, and at the summit an octagonal guard room covered with a vault thick enough to bear the weight of artillery. Both towers have a main stair rising the full height from courtyard to parapet and a second stair leading upward from the curtain wall-walk allowing circulation of the battlements, still enjoyed by visitors today, without going through the rooms. Guy's Tower probably stands on the site of a smaller 13th century tower probably round in plan.

The Clock Tower or gatehouse is a square building with round turrets towards the field and octagonal turrets to the court. There are three suites of lodgings over the rib-vaulted entrance passage which is closed by a portcullis with murder holes behind. There is another portcullis in the barbican in front of the gate which is partly open to the sky, whilst the other part has two storeys of lodgings over the passage and polygonal turrets facing the ditch on either side. the walls of the gatehouse and barbican are a maze of stairs, passages, and small bedchambers so although the building looks impressive from the outside there is actually very little of solid walling. Accurate artillery fire would have rapidly reduced it to ruin. Indeed the whole NE front, although almost impregnable to infantry, was evidently built as much for show as for defence.

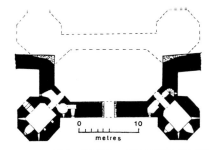

ICHARD III'S TOWER, WARWICK CASTLE

PLAN OF THE EAST GATE

East Gate
of Warwick
Town Wall

The curtain wall SW of Guy's Tower is the same height as on the NE front and although it may contain an earlier core is essentially of the same build. The rest of the western side from there to the mound had 19th century parapets at a much lower level and there is doubt as to whether this portion ever rose any higher. Much of the walling is thin 18th century work and there is a wide and high arch through it, although on the bank alongside it are fragments of what may be the original curtain of c1180 which was here never rebuilt. Projecting from this side is the outer part of the basement of the tower house begun by Richard III and left unfinished probably at about its present height at his death in 1485. Probably at least three or four more storeys were planned to bring it up to about the height of Guy's Tower and it would have been a self contained unit with its own water supply, cellars, and kitchen. It was 23.2m long by about 13m wide over walling up to 2.6m thick and had octagonal corner towers 7.5m in diameter containing rectangular rooms having round gunports. The doorway between the two surviving towers known as the Clarence Tower and Bear Tower is modern. The inner portion towards the courtyard stood when Robert Smythson made a plan of the castle for Fulke Greville in the 1590s but was probably pulled down soon afterwards to provide materials for the new apartments.

The town of Warwick was fortified by Ethelfleda in c909 so the ditch which William I ordered Turchil of Arden to construct perhaps followed a similar line to an older one. In places the ditch had to be cut into the sandstone and when a stone wall was built probably in the 13th century it rose directly from the inner face. There was a grant of murage for upkeep in 1305, and two of the 15th century Earls intended to rebuild the wall but presumably failed to do so. It was then already falling down and little remained for Leland to see c1540. Only short and partly rebuilt sections now remain north of each of the East and West Gates. The West Gate was rebuilt c1370 and extended westwards in the early 15th century to provide a base for a tower to be added to the church of St James above it. In the 15th century the East Gate was rebuilt and St Peter's Chapel built above it. In the 1780s the gate was refaced and the chapel rebuilt. The North Gate mentioned in 1272 vanished before Leland's time.

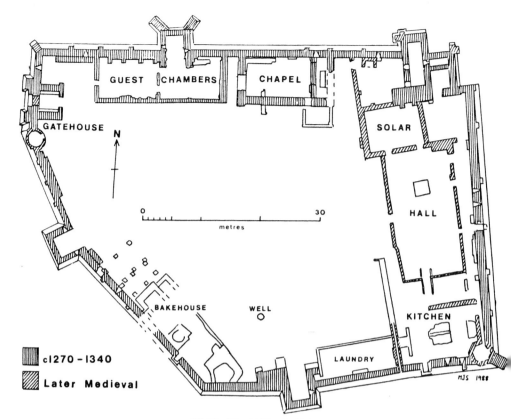

PLAN OF WEOLEY CASTLE

Labels within plan: GUEST CHAMBERS, CHAPEL, GATEHOUSE, N, SOLAR, HALL, BAKEHOUSE, WELL, KITCHEN, LAUNDRY, metres, 0, 30, MJS 1988

Legend: c1270-1340 / Later Medieval

WEOLEY CASTLE

SP 022827

Weoley belonged to William FitsAnsculf, Lord of Dudley, when the Domesday Survey was made in 1086. It passed through his daughter to the Paganels, who built the first series of timber buildings on a moated platform rather smaller than the present one. Late in the 12th century the manor passed to Roger de Somery, and either he or his son Ralph appear to have built a stone hall on the eastern part of the site. Ralph's son Roger was in 1267 licensed by Henry III to build stone walls and fortifications, and the present walls and towers are thought to have been built in the 1270s, the enclosed area extending further west than the original platform did. Later in this period a new stone hall and stone barn were added.

When Sir John de Somery died in 1322 Weoley went to his sister Joan, married to Thomas Botetort. They and their successors built another barn, the chapel, and the garderobe system in the NE corner. In 1384 the heiress Joyce de Botetort brought Weoley to Sir Hugh de Burnell, who held it until 1430, and probably built a structure on the west side of the court. In 1439 the manor descended to the Berkeleys, who were attainted by Henry VII in 1485 as supporters of the vanquished Richard III, and they were replaced by the Dudleys. They sold Weoley to Richard Jerveys, Sheriff of London, in 1536, and his descendants held it until the early 19th century, although the castle was ruined by the mid 17th century, and does not appear to have taken part in the Civil War.

The castle has a low lying site beside a stream and for defence much reliance must have been placed on a wide wet moat. By the 20th century the buildings had crumbled away almost down to courtyard level and were covered with silt and debris. Little architecturally was known of them prior to a long series of excavations started in the 1930s, and continuing up until 1962. Despite the loss of early excavation reports in a fire during the War, it has been possible to reconstruct most of the history of the site.

In plan the castle is very roughly a rectangle 75m long by 60m wide with the SW corner canted off. The surrounding wall averaged 1.2m thick above a broad battered plinth rising from the bottom of the moat, and had thin decorative pilaster buttresses at intervals. There are small square towers at the NE corner, in the middle of the north, south, and SW sides, and in the west wall near the NW corner, the latter also being the gateway until blocked up later. Before the walls existed the access to the platform was by a timber bridge on the east, and the present access by a causeway on the SW side has no precedent historically speaking.

The NE tower stands by a pit for garderobes for the solar to the south, beyond which was the later timber hall, with in the SE corner the hearths of a kitchen. The earlier stone hall remains underlie the north end of the later one and the solar block. On the SE was a small polygonal turret, perhaps of the late 14th century, and there is a second round turret corbelled out of the corner by the former gatehouse. On the north side of the court are buildings which from the detailed description of the castle made in 1424 can be deduced to be the guest apartments and chapel respectively. On the SW side are ovens and bakehouses, and between the south tower and kitchen are stone footings for a timber framed laundry block.

The NE corner of Weoley Castle

WHICHFORD CASTLE

SP 308346

King John gave Whichford to Reynold de Mohun in 1204 and probably his descendants built the castle in the early 14th century. In 1405 it passed to Richard, Lord Strange, and in the early 16th century it went to the Stanleys. Whichford was sold to the Sheldons in the early 17th century and to the Philips's c1820. Immediately west of the village is a platform 60m square surrounded by a wet moat held in on the east by an outer bank. There are causeways across the moat on the north and south. Neither are likely to be original.

WHITACRE HALL

SP 242937

The hall is an L-shaped house rebuilt in the 18th century except for the 17th century back wing. It lies within a nearly square wet moat with a stone inner lining flanked at each corner except the NE by a square sandstone tower with a loop in each wall and having a tiny late 16th century gatehouse on the south side. Whitacre was held in the late 13th century by Robert Marmion but the defences are likely to be the work of Ralph Basset of Drayton to whom the manor was leased and then finally conveyed in 1320. It was later associated with the de Birminghams, Whittacres, Ferrers, Chetwynds, Devereux, Longevilles, and Cheneys, and in 1542 was leased to John Starkey.

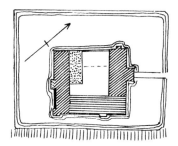

BADDESLEY CLINTON

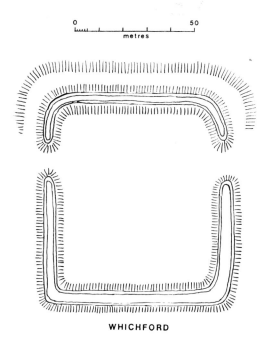

0   50
metres

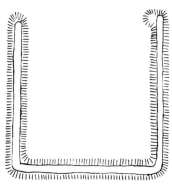

HONILEY

WHICHFORD

PLANS OF MOATED SITES

54

A SELECTED LIST OF OTHER MOATED SITES

ADMINGTON SP 205464 Shallow dry moat around platform 24m square.
ARLEY HALL SP 277905 Traces of former moat to the west.
BAXTERLEY SP 256970 3m deep dry moat with causeway to SE around an
  overgrown platform 45m by 30m. Former seat of the Chetwynds.
BENTLEY SP 280961 Shallow nearly dry moat. Platform 45m by 30m.
BERRY HALL SP 191792 Fine 16th century half timbered house within
  a moat about 43m by 40m still wet except on the east side.
BINLEY SP 370776 Platform with deep, partly wet, moat by school.
BLOSSOMFIELD SP 148787 Small enclosure with moat still wet on east.
BOCKENDON GRANGE SP 279760 Wet moat to NE. Second moat to west.
BROME COURT SP 088526 Two and a half sides of a wet moat to east.
BROME HALL SP 184705 Remains of moat to NE. Belonged to the Bromes,
  and then, in the 16th century, the Catesbys.
CALDECOTE SP 342948 Half of a rectangular wet moat WSW of church.
CALUDON SP 374799 A dry rectangular moat lies south of the castle.
CAROL GREEN SP 253777 Part of a dry moat remains around a house.
COLESHILL SP 192884 Signs of moat to NE of Hall Farm.
COTON SP 518796 Grange of Combe Abbey. Held by Dixwells 1540-1757.
  Moat could be of either period. Present house is later.
DORSINGTON SP 134497 Overgrown moat, nearly dry, around house.
DRAKENAGE SP 223953 Moat north of farm. Probably site of Mancester
  family house. Later passed to the Herles and de Hastings.
EARLSWOOD COURT SP 124742 Three sides of narrow moat around an area
  of irregular shape 0.6km north of Court. 2nd moat near station.
EASTCOTE HALL SP 191792 A wet moat surrounds the house, which looks
  Victorian, but has remains of a genuine 15th century hall.
FULFORD HEATH SP 097744 Part of moat in field near Earlswood Lakes.
GOODREST SP 274699 Moat, still wet on north side, around house.
GRIFF SP 357892 Little remains of the moat of the Sudeleys' house.
GROVE PARK SP 237649 Basement of 1830 house looks onto moat. Held
  by the Hastings and Beauchamp families in the 14th century.
HENWOOD SP 188783 Irregularly shaped platform 35m by 25m within wet
  moat with adjoining pool to SE. By junction of stream & R.Blythe.
HERMITAGE SP 233856 Moat around farm, still water filled on east.
HEYGATE SP 053981 This rectangular dry moat near to a house may be
  a relic of Sir Robert Stephenson's house in the 14th century.
HONILEY SP 242731 Three sides of a wet moat. Enclosure 55m square.
HOLLYBERRY END SP 265841 Part of an irregularly shaped wet moat.
KINWARTON SP 106586 Moat north of 14th century dovecot. Held by the
  de Brulys from Evesham Abbey. Later house built by Hopkins.
LAPWORTH PARK SP 168707 37m square platform. Well preserved moat.
LIGHT HALL FARM SP 123769 Half remains of wet moat up to 20m wide.
MAXSTOKE SP 235867 Moat around house to south of the priory ruins.
MERIDEN SP 242811 Slight traces of rectangular moat in field.
MIDDLETON SP 194982 House of various periods including one Norman
  window. Moat to north. Founded by the Marmions. Baldwin Freville
  licenced to have private chapel 1390. Later held by Binghams.
MOAT HOUSE FARM SP 220861 Part of wet moat to NW of the house.
MOUNT PLEASANT SP 127669 Three sides of a wet moat in a garden.
NORTH WOOD SP 192960 Moat hidden in woodland.
OLDFIELD SP 214684 Nearly dry moat, now overgrown.
OLD MOATHOUSE SP 117734 Very narrow wet moat around house.
OVER GREEN SP 167944 A large fragmentary rectangular wet moat.
PACKWOOD SP 169728 Wet moat 10m wide around platform of 80m by 60m
  around house west of church. Smaller moat 1km to SW.
PARK FARM SP 383848 Remains of moat to west and north of farm.
PEDDIMORE HALL SP 154937 Rectangular wet moat around farmhouse and
  remains of concentric outer moat to north and west.

PINLEY SP 215657 Large moat to south and east of Abbey. The family
   of the last Abbess, Margaret Wigston, got it at the Dissolution.
SIDENHALES SP 138751 A pool and two partly wet arms of the moat
   remain behind the farmhouse.
STIVICHALL SP 317757 A square moat, now dry, but with a pool at a
   corner, lies by the Coventry Performing Arts Centre.
STOCKTON SP 439635 Three sides of a wet moat south of the church.
STONETON SP 464546 Manor house within moat, wet on north side.
STOURTON SP 297370 Feint traces of moat 145m by 40m by stream.
UMBERSLADE SP 137208 Overgrown dry moat. Platform 35m square.
WIGSTON HILL SP 273963 One side of wet moat to west of a house.
WILLOUGHBY SP 516673 Rectangular wet moat south of the church.
WOOD END SP 102718 Overgrown wet moat in midst of a golf course.
WYKE SP 073607 Partly wet moat of platform 48m by 43m damaged by a
   lane across it. Held by de Coctons & de Brulys in 13th century.

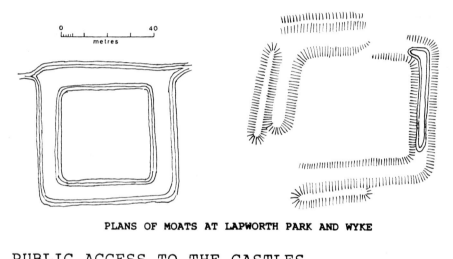

PLANS OF MOATS AT LAPWORTH PARK AND WYKE

PUBLIC ACCESS TO THE CASTLES

Fee Payable: Warwick, Weoley, Kenilworth, Coughton, Baddesley Clinton
Free access at any time: Beaudesert, Brailes, Brinklow, Caludon,
   Fillingley, Seckington, Warwick & Coventry town gateways.
Alongside public roads, footpaths, churchyards, etc: Astley, Hobbs,
   Hartshill, Kingsbury, moats at Baxterley, Billesley, and Wyke.

Some of the castles and moated mansions described and illustrated
in this book also appear in an earlier volume of this series called
The Castles and Moated Mansions of Staffordshire & The West Midlands
County which was published in March 1989 and is now nearing the end
of the print run. It was felt preferable to revert to the pre-1974
boundary for this volume. The material for Staffordshire as it was
before the boundary changes will probably be re-issued with extra
illustrations at some point in the future.

Other castle volumes of this series now in preparation include:
Ireland, Clydeside, Dumfries and Galloway, and Yorkshire.
If you wish to be informed when any of these are released ask to be
included on the Folly Publications mailing list. Send your address
to Folly Cottage, 151 West Malvern Road, Malvern, Worcs, WR14 4AY.